Sweet Innocent Naive

A Reflection on Life and Experiencing God

SHERRIE A. HILL, D. MIN.

LAEL PUBLISHING

Sweet Innocent Naive

A Reflection on Life and Experiencing God
by Sherrie A. Hill, D. Min.
Published by The Lael Agency
Winston Salem, North Carolina
www.LaelAgency.com

No part of this book may be used or reproduced in any form, stored in a retrieval system, or transmitted in any form by any means, electronic, photocopy, mechanical, recording or otherwise without written permission from the author. The only exception is for critical articles or reviews, in which brief excerpts may be used.

Paperback ISBN - 978-1-7325344-8-3
Hardback ISBN - 978-1-7325344-9-0

Inside Illustrations:
Michelle Tran

Author's Photo:
Bobby and Freda Edwards

Author's contact:
Email: MayHill107@aol.com
Website: SherrieAHill.com

Copyright © 2020 by Dr. Sherrie A. Hill, D. Min.

All Rights Reserved

First Edition

Printed in the United States of America.

Dedication

To God, for had it not been for Him, I would not have survived and grown spiritually from the experiences described in this book. To Him for whispering to me my heavenly name, "Sariba," which means Woman of Grace and Favor. For the courage and healing and comfort that God restored in me once again to commence writing this book. Thank you, God, and I love you.

To my parents, Bishop Johnny L. Hill, Sr. and Evangelist Helen A. Hill, for the spiritual seeds they placed within me – nurturing me, fasting and praying for me, caring for me, loving me, and giving of themselves to God and to me. Both are now with the Lord (2012…2014) and I know that they are rejoicing with me for the completion of this book. Thank you, mom and dad, and until we meet again, I love you.

To my grandparents, who are both with the Lord (1999….1987) Bishop Albert Hill, Sr. and Mother Artelia Hill, who shared the truth with me, during one of the most difficult times in my life. Thank you, ma and grandpa, and until we meet again, I love you.

Acknowledgements

To my sister, Gwen, who was always lifting me up during the good, the bad, and the ugly times in my life. I am so appreciative of your calls during the times when I needed a word from the Lord, the encouragement you gave me to keep going forward and not get stuck in this endeavor, and additionally, the financial blessings you sent to me when I least expected it. I love you.

To my brother Johnny for encouraging me to open up my heart and try love again after a devastating relationship experience. To my brothers Stephen and Alex, who always had their protective eyes on me. I love you all.

To my spiritual parents, Bishop James and Joyce Hash, for their spiritual covering and continued prayers over me, especially now that my parents are with the Lord. I love you both.

Endorsements

"Reading this book is like taking a journey with a typical "preacher's kid" who experienced real life without the benefit of a Real Life 101 preparation manual. Her insightful diagram of landmarks in her journey of being reconciled with Christ is worth the whole book. I have no doubt that Sweet, Innocent, and Naive (SIN) will help other women of faith on their journeys towards a deeper and more complete faith."

Shirley P. Carter
Financial Services
Dixon, Hughes, Goodman, LLP

"Bishop and I realized after reading your book, that you have experienced a great deal of pain during this challenging period of your life.

It is our desire that your book will be an enlightenment to young ladies who are experiencing or have experienced similar encounters of the enemy.

Thanks to God you are a living testimony to the power of prayer, and now have overcome the attacks of Satan. May this book be a beacon to all your readers.

We are honored by the opportunity to endorse your book."

Drs. Leonard and Martha H. Goode
Faith United COLG

"What an awesome book – I had no idea you had accomplished so much. I am in awe of you and what God has done in your life. You are definitely an instrument of his Glory to be shared with the world. There is no power stronger than the human spirit when it is set on fire by the Holy Spirit. Flame On, my sister, Flame On!!! An inspiring, personal story of disappointments, struggles, and ultimately victory, Sweet, Innocent, Naive is a testament that the easiest place to be a Christian is when you are in church."

James R. Gorham
Brigadier General (Ret.)
Author of *Sharecropper's Wisdom,*
Growing Today's Leaders the Old-Fashioned Way

"I look at your book as a very powerful, personal testimony from a loving, Christ-centered woman who is not ashamed to glorify God. I believe your testimony will touch many, especially the lost young girls and ladies out there who feel "hopeless and helpless" based on beliefs gained fromthe lies of the enemy.

I thank God for healing you and giving you courage to glorify Him through your pain. I often think of Hebrew 2:18 (NIV) in terms of the Great I AM who has suffered but endured and thus, giving us hope to look at our situation/s through His eyes. When we do that, then we can claim that "ALL THINGS WORK TOGETHER FOR

GOOD, TO THOSE WHO LOVE THE LORD AND ARE CALLED ACCORDING TO HIS PURPOSE" Rom 8:28 (KJV)."

Dr. Ben Omungu, Ph.D
Owner & Director, Covenant Counseling Center

"Perhaps the most pressing and important job that we have today is preparing our girls for the world they will face as adults...

It is with special pride that I am able to offer a few words about the book you have written. It was a compilation of words that served to summon every emotion in my being. Had I not known you prior to reading your prose, I certainly would have felt a bond with you by the conclusion. Not only did you report the facts, but you also got to the very essence of who you are and were as a young African-American woman and preacher's daughter, trying to navigate your life while keeping God first, even though the devil was busy.

Language is powerful. The misuse of words has launched wars; the appropriate use could author peace in the world. There were times when I wanted to give you the right words to say to characters in your book, from your ex-boyfriend/future husband to your camp directors. Your words will serve to assist many as they begin the next steps in their lives.

I commend your prescience in recognizing and claiming

the jewel that is you, Dr. Sherrie Hill. (aka Baby Girl)"

Johanna L. Wright
Educator/Coach
Retired

Contents

Foreword 15

Introduction 17

Chapter 1- Sweet Innocent Naïve Sin 21

Chapter 2- The Prom 27

Chapter 3- The Dreaded 12-Inch Wooden Ruler 39

Chapter 4- Barbeque Restaurant 43

Chapter 5- Leaving For College 51

Chapter 6- A Life-Changing Experience 55

Chapter 7- Graz, Austria 61

Chapter 8- German Street Car Experience 69

Chapter 9- Day in the Sun 73

Chapter 10- Opera in Vienna 77

Chapter 11- Defeating the Challenge 81

Chapter 12- Life after the Graz, Austria Adventure 89

Chapter 13- Sex before Marriage? 95

Chapter 14- Cape Hatteras 101

Chapter 15- Fair Exchange for Voice Lessons 113

Chapter 16- Surprise Birthday Dinner 121

Contents

Chapter 17 - Eye of the Hurricane..................... 125

Chapter 18 - Attack of the Devil......................... 135

Chapter 19 - Encounter with Good & Evil.......... 141

Chapter 20 - Christmas Morning........................ 143

Chapter 21 - Undergraduate Graduation............ 147

Chapter 22 - Home for the Summer.................... 149

Chapter 23 - Destiny Killer................................. 151

Chapter 24 - Love and Graduate School............. 157

Chapter 25 - Letting Go...................................... 165

Scriptures and Spiritual Journal
    What to Do When Trouble Hits Your Life...... 171

Foreword

While the Bible clearly shows that temptation is not itself sin (Heb. 4:15), this life account reminds us that even if one is "sweet," "innocent," and "naïve," the tempter has a way of dangling the enticement in front of us that leads to sin. In an effort to help others, Sherrie Hill has opened her heart and life to her readers to serve both as a warning and as an encouragement: a warning that reminds all of us who have been raised in the church that we are not above falling; an encouragement that no matter where temptation takes us, repentance before God is the only way to reclaim a right standing with Him through the shed blood of Jesus Christ.

As unique creations of our Heavenly Father, each of our stories is different. The point of this treatise is not to emphasize those experiences that are different, nor to glorify the accomplishments of an individual, but rather, to provide a window into those common elements of life that can become so challenging. As readers look through these windows, they will find within these pages a sequence of mirrors that allow them to reflect on their own lives and life choices.

Life can often make one hard, critical, and cynical. At times, people can look back and yearn for that time when one was sweet, innocent, and naïve. Rather than yearning for what we are not, this book helps the reader to find that no matter what happens in life, and no matter where our choices lead, a tender heart before God is achievable – and should be the ultimate goal of all of His children.

Dr. John L. Lindsey
Dean, School of Ministry John Wesley University

    Singleness is not depicted in a good light within our present society. Society inflicts weariness and great pressures on individuals both single and married. Thus, individuals feel the impulsive need to connect and conjoin with persons who have no fulfilled purpose within their lives. However, this book Sweet Innocent Naïve (SIN) can be a breath of fresh air for the discouraged and disheartened, for believers and non-believers alike, who feel trapped in a mundane and mediocre existence.

    Sherrie's insight in this book is the perfect prescription to inject new life and hope into fatigued hearts, infuse fresh excitement and meaning into ordinary lives, and lift readers into higher realms of realized potential and fulfillment of God's purpose in their lives. A great, inspiring book to read.

Bishop James C. Hash, Sr.
Senior Pastor and CEO
St. Peter's Church and World Outreach Center

Introduction

Sweet **I**nnocent **N**aive

S I N

I began writing on August 11, 2002, but I found that I was not emotionally ready yet. God told me that to write is to heal and therefore, I received a Rhema Word, which is a Word from God. I knew within my heart it was time for me to start writing this book, which contains personal experiences. I've never been someone who openly talked about myself, but if what I share will help someone else, then I am compelled to write. This book for those who either have or are suffering in their lives, to let them know that God will never allow us to bear any more than we can handle. Our trials and tribulations exist to make us who God created us to be, not who society, family, or friends say we are. When God said, "Let There Be," He wanted that person He created to come forth and be the man or woman He had in mind.

By the blood of Jesus, I pray that this book will be a blessing to all who read it. It is not a book of fiction, but a book of real-life experiences suffered, endured, and overcome as pure gold.

While I was living in Nashville, Tennessee in 1999,

God told me to write about my experiences. I shared that inspired word with a couple of friends, but I procrastinated for a while. Meanwhile I relocated back to North Carolina in 2001, and I received a "prophecy" confirming my assignment to write a book about my experiences again in 2002 by a minister I'd never met before. He even described the type of notebooks I should purchase to begin writing down my experiences in the form of a journal. This prophet also described the sick feeling I had been experiencing within my stomach that I had never shared with anyone else. He informed me that the sick feeling was not from something I had eaten but from the need to write this book. This confirming prophet's words were correct, and he was indeed a true prophet who was a total stranger to me, but truly heard from God. I was so amazed, because very few people knew that I'd said that the Lord told me while living in TN to write a book about my life experiences.

After this experience, I finally stopped procrastinating and went out on August 11, 2002and purchased the 3 notebooks the prophet said to purchase. When I went to the store and located the notebook shelf, there were only 3 notebooks left in the first bend that I put my hand on. I knew that was more confirmation for me to write. With the notebooks, I purchased a small bottle of lemonade to drink, which made the bill a total of $3.37. To me scripturally the #3 translates to the Father, Son, and Holy Ghost and the #7 translates to God's perfect will & completion. 3+7=10.

To me scripturally, the #10 translates to ordain of God.

It is my belief that it's ordained by God that I write this book. I asked God to help me because I didn't know how to even start. God said to take one experience of your life at a time and you will not get overwhelmed. Some of my experiences I would like to simply forget about, but we do not go through experiences of trials and tribulation for ourselves. We go through them and overcome them to grow in our faith in God and to help others learn how to do the same by sharing our experiences.

I pray that the anointing of God will fall on those who read this book, that they will be changed forever and blessed by what they read. Some might ask the question… "What's so special about these experiences?" I knew that you would ask me that question. The answer is, these were my experiences and I received a Rhema Word from the Lord to write about them as I remembered them. Therefore, I simply trust in God that He has a purpose beyond my understanding, and I act in obedience on what He has instructed me to do. Obedience is always better than sacrifice.

I asked God what title I should use for this book and the following words entered my spirit. The title SWEET, INNOCENT, AND NAÏVE, as you cast your eyes on the first letters of each word; they are the acronym for the word "SIN." We can be sweet, innocent, and naïve, but still sin in many forms.

Chapter 1

Sweet Innocent Naive
SIN

No matter what man says, wait to have sex if you are not married. I was born and raised in a Christian family; my father, mother, and grandfather were ministers of the Gospel of the Pentecostal Church organization and therefore, I did not have the typical lifestyle of a teenager. Our public-school teachers and friends in the community of our small Southern town knew our families to be Christian families. We were treated with the highest level of respect because of this standing. As a teenager, I was only exposed to attending church, school, shopping, and working when I became old enough to get a job. My older sister started working at our uncles' restaurant, but I was too young to work there so I cleaned my uncle and aunt's home to make some money because our parents believed that we should learn how to work and save our own money as soon as possible. It taught us responsibility and independence.

I began dating in the 10th grade, a very intelligent handsome 6'1" young man with nice broad muscular shoulders, beautiful brown eyes, and a very deep sexy voice similar to that of R & B singer Barry White. It was a voice that would make any young girl feel like she was melting when she heard it; it would make her heart start beating faster than normal or make her liver quiver.

Dating in our home, according to my parents, meant not going to the movies, zero intimacy with the opposite sex, not going to football games, and not attending basketball games. What it did include was going to church, eating out, and being home by 10:00p.m. Due to the fact that I understood our household rules and always followed them to the very letter, I was always frightened to have sex as a Christian young lady. This was based on hearing about other young ladies getting in trouble, and even the church environment treating them as though they were the stinky, dirty scum of the earth and no one should be around them. But I also saw that the young man's life would just continue as though nothing happened. I was fearful that I would get pregnant if I allowed sex in the relationship and would be treated in the same cruel manner by others. Therefore, my first dating experiences only included talking a lot at school, at church, and by telephone. In my mind as well as in his, this was acceptable because he was also from a well-respected Christian family. He never pressured me for anything else because he knew my family's definition of the word "dating" in our household. He also had to receive permission from my parents to date me, before any type of dating took place.

The day he was scheduled to come to our home to ask for permission to date me was similar to a young man asking a girl's father for permission for his daughters' hand in marriage. This was a very serious task that had to be completed before any dating me could take place.

The meeting was scheduled for 3:00 p.m. on a Saturday. The doorbell rang at 2:50 p.m. My father answered the door and escorted him into the living room. My mother and I entered the room. My mother spoke and sat next to my father on the sofa directly in front of him while I sat in the chair next to him. I took one look at him and smiled; I've never seen a man sweat so badly from being nervous. As he spoke with my parents, his voice began to shake: sweat was popping off of his forehead, his hands were sweaty and shaking, his shirt was wet, and he looked as though he was going to pass out from the fear of my mother. He had told me earlier that he felt very comfortable being around my father but he was terrified of my mother, and he didn't think she liked him when he'd see her out at the grocery store or just out around town.

The dating rules were now in place, accepted, and

permission was granted. As he took his handkerchief out of his pocket, I offered him a cold glass of water; he was so relieved that he asked for a second glass. He was always a gentleman when he was in my presence, always treated me with respect because he knew my family were Christians; some members of his family were also Christians. In fact, some of his family members attended the same church as my family.

As we began the dating game, some of our times together included riding through downtown in his cute VW; malls did not exist at this time in our lives. We enjoyed going to the local state park, watching the kids play on the merry-go-round, and seeing the black and yellow feathered butterflies fly from one plant to another. The sky was such a beautiful clear blue, and the weather was similar to a day in the Bahamas, only without the ocean. I would enjoy him pushing the back of my swing as high as it could go as I held on as tight as possible with the wind blowing past my face. Many times, we would have lunch on Saturdays at Shoney's, enjoying eating our favorite strawberry pie. We would discuss his plans for attending college or joining a branch of the military. I recommended that he attend a nearby college or university and I would assist him with the research to determine which option would be the best. I was afraid of him joining the army or any branch of the military due to the lack of safety in enemy territory.

We attended church together even though he did

not seem to enjoy it as much due to the type of church environment, because this was a Holy Ghost-filled, fire-baptized, tongue-speaking, running, and shouting church. He was Mr. Cool. Therefore, he would attend but he was not a participant. I remember myself not being much of a participant when he would attend. Now that I think about it, was I beginning to put him first instead of God being first the way He had been before this young man entered my life?

That can be so easy to do when you are caught up in your emotions. I remember not being very attentive to the preacher's sermon because I was so delighted that he was there with me, while in my mind it looked really good to my parents that he was in church. Instead of my being a participant in church, I became a spectator when he was with me.

Is there a person, place, or thing that has your attention so that you cannot hear the word of God?

Stay focused on God and His Word.

Chapter 2

The Prom

I was scheduled to graduate from high school in 1974 but God blessed me to test out and leave high school without graduating. I completely skipped the twelfth grade. This was called early college admittance, which meant I was leaving for college one year earlier than my classmates. This practice was really unheard of in our small Southern town, and therefore his senior year in high school became my senior year too instead of my junior year in high school. We were now planning to end our last year by attending high school prom. My mother, an expert seamstress, spent many hours creating a beautiful Vogue-patterned gown for my first and last high school prom. My gown was a beautiful peach-colored floor length dress, soft chiffon and silk fabric with rhinestones trimmed around the midriff area of the dress with a long shawl trimmed with rhinestones to match. I wore rhinestone earrings; the shoes were dyed peach trimmed with rhinestones to match my dress. My hair was up in curls with bangs and a small tiara similar to the hairstyle worn by Audrey Hepburn in the movie Breakfast at Tiffany's. Needless to say, I looked and felt a little like a princess. I was so excited about going to the prom, my body felt like I was going to burst like a blown-up balloon that gets busted when you've blown it up too much and it pops.

All my girlfriends who were still juniors in high school were getting ready for the prom with their senior high school boyfriends as well. Everyone was making plans for dinner either before or after the prom. I only listened to my girlfriends talking about going to the prom with their boyfriends and making plans for their big prom night. I never said anything specifically to my girlfriends about my plans because with my boyfriend's history of tardiness or not showing up as planned, I was not certain I would make it to the prom. In order to keep from embarrassing myself and boasting like my girlfriends, I kept quiet and left the plans up to my boyfriend. I was secretly stressing out and hoping in my heart that I was going to even get to the prom, given his history of not showing up. According to him, there was always a good reason for him not showing up for our scheduled dates or being very late. I always accepted his excuses even though each time it caused me a great deal of stress because punctuality was always important to me but never to him.

    The day of the prom was very beautiful. The sun was bright, the sky was blue, and birds were chirping. Earlier that day, I had gotten a manicure and pedicure. I took a long bubble bath and used some of my mother's expensive Boucheron perfume. I sat in my bedroom in my robe and listened to soft music until it was time to get dressed for our big night. I was so very calm, peaceful, and relaxed; one would have thought that I had just had a professional full-body massage. When I looked at the clock it was about 6:00 p.m. and time to get dressed in my beautiful gown that my mother had spent many hours creating for me. My boyfriend was scheduled to arrive at 7:30 p.m. I finished dressing and went to the living room to wait for his arrival. I'd asked him earlier that day, to please be on time.

    As I sat on the sofa and waited for his arrival, I could just imagine him ringing the doorbell. My dad would answer the door and he would walk into the living room wearing his black tuxedo and bow tie. He would gently place the wrist corsage, which I'd requested he purchase to match my peach evening gown, on my wrist. He would tell me how beautiful I looked and I would tell him how handsome he looked as he escorted me to his car and opened the door as a gentlemen does. I then imagined the two of us arriving to the prom, walking in the double doors just like a prince and princess with everyone staring, like one would stare at Cinderella and her Prince. And people would say to themselves, what an awesome looking couple as we walked down the stairs entering the ballroom. I imagined that the lights would be turned down low in the room to give it a more romantic atmosphere; soft music would be playing, and the spotlight would be shining on just the two of us.

As I glanced at the clock sitting on the living room table, I saw that the time was now 7:15 p.m. Once again, I imagined my girlfriends being jealous and envious of what they were seeing as we walked into the ballroom because I was sure that some of them did not think I was going to make it to the prom, based on my boyfriend's history. Again, I glanced at the clock and saw that the time was now 7:25 p.m. I began to smile and feel all warm and fuzzy inside, because I knew he would be arriving very soon. At 7:30 p.m., I thought heard his VW pull up in front of our house, but the sound of the car kept going down the street and did not stop. I looked at the clock again; it was now 8:00 p.m., and in my heart, I was starting to feel a small amount of stress. Several cars had passed by and none of them were his VW, which meant that I was waiting and waiting and still waiting for him to show up. I got up from the sofa and moved to the chair as my father came in the living room to ask if he had called. I answered very quietly, not yet. My brother was also going to the prom with his girlfriend and he had already left several hours ago while I was still waiting to get to my big night. My mother came into the living room to tell me how beautiful I looked, offering me subtle words of encouragement as I continued to wait. The clock was now showing 9:00 p.m. and I was about to burst from the stress of waiting. The beautiful night that I'd imagined was now fast turning into a downhill rollercoaster ride of sheer anger, disgust, hurt, and disappointment. The many hours my mother had spent on creating this beautiful evening gown was beginning to feel like wasted time, money, and energy. I was feeling so much stress that I wanted to scream at the top of my voice. Inside my mind, I was feeling like an emotional wreck, but I never displayed my emotions to my parents because that would just be another strike against him, especially with my mother. I hated the fact that once again on such a major event, he did not come through for me. He had once again hurt and embarrassed me and because of that, I was becoming more hurt and angrier with him by the second.

At 9:25 p.m. I was still sitting in my dress waiting. In the past my father had never said anything directly to me or to him but I knew that my mother was not very happy with his habits of disappointing me, as he had done so many times in the past. I began thinking to myself, please, not again, especially on this very important night. His not showing up was really causing me more stress because I knew what my mother was thinking and feeling but not saying to me: that this young man had once again disappointed her precious sweet, innocent, and naive daughter.

Just as I'd decided he was not going to come, and I was mentally preparing that it was time to take my beautiful dress and shoes off, the doorbell rang! It was 9:30 p.m., and he was finally here. Of course, he had an excuse for being late, not even one that I can remember right now. Even though I was angry, disgusted, hurt, and stressed, I kept my emotions to myself. I decided to go with him anyway because I was glad that my mother was not disappointed with his habit of being late or not showing up with a sorry excuse once again. Neither did I have to defend him again even though his excuses were not acceptable. I made the decision that the beautiful dress my mother had created for me with her time, money, and energy was not going to be wasted.

He entered our living room, not in a black tuxedo with a black bow tie, but a regular grey suit with a white shirt and gray and black suit tie that he had worn to church. I was pleased, though, that he did have with him the wrist corsage that matched my dress, as I had requested earlier during the week.

My father reminded him that my curfew was 12:00 midnight. As he escorted me out of the front door down our walkway to the car, I looked up and it was not his VW, a cozy little car for just the two of us, but a big white Ford

Sedan that also had a male friend of ours sitting in the back seat wearing a pair of brown pants, a plaid shirt, no tie, and white tennis shoes, chewing bubble gum and talking a mile a minute. I could feel my blood pressure rising and a headache approaching. I immediately became even more discouraged, realizing that I was not going to be the girl who walks in the door of the prom with just the two of us, like many of my girlfriends were going to do with their dates.

My dream prom night totally vanished in my heart. Even though he showed up late, I was still not his priority the way I had imagined I was going to be on such a special night for a young girl. My heart was already heavy and hurting, similar to a person grieving the death of a loved one, because he was late, he was not wearing a nice black tuxedo with a black bow tie as we'd discussed, he arrived with a male friend of ours sitting in the back seat of the car also not appropriately dressed and chewing bubble gum, and he had truly destroyed my dream of entering the prom ballroom on his arm like a queen just as I knew my friends would be doing. It also hurt my heart because once again, my mother was disappointed in his habitual tardiness and lame excuses. My heart so deeply wanted this night to be special and to feel like I was really important to him, to simply feel like I was his priority. But once again, being his priority did not happen.

Even then I was very good at hiding my feelings and

therefore, I made a decision not to share with him nor anyone else what I was really feeling. To be very honest, I really wanted to pick something up and hit him with it and tell him to just leave. Certain words came to mind but none a young girl from a devout Christian family could verbalize. I'd only heard my friends use stronger words to really make a very important point in their conversations. In my family, thought, we could not even think such words, much less say them to someone. Hitting someone was also something I could not do because I could have gone to jail. Violence did not exist in my family, but that was the intense inner level of stress that he had psychologically driven me to with his past and current behavior.

Since this was now also my senior prom, I decided to just try to get through the rest of this already horrible night. We arrived at the prom with our third person tagging along wearing his white tennis shoes to a black-tie event, still chewing and popping bubble gum while talking a mile a minute about nothing to my boyfriend.

As the three of us_walked in the gym, I noticed that it had been so beautifully decorated with flowers and ribbons. People were standing around the room chatting with each other, girls wearing gowns of all lengths and in all the colors of the rainbow, but we noticed that no one was dancing on the dance floor. But the guys seemed to be angry, and some of the girls were standing around crying. We were puzzled and started inquiring what was

The Prom

going on. We were informed that the band for the prom had not shown up. We could not get the details about why the band did not show up, but everyone was very upset and disappointed because their big prom night had been ruined.

Needless to say, that bit of bad news really made me feel better because I was not the only person disappointed for the big prom night. Everyone else had also experienced a sense of anger and disappointment. I was no longer alone with a heavy heart for the night. While I stood by watching and in sheer disbelief at the scene, my boyfriend and our third person spent a few more minutes talking with others about what could have happened to the band. I looked at my watch and reminded my boyfriend that it was time for me to be taken back home because I had a 12:00 midnight curfew. The time was 11:30 p.m. and too late for him to take me out to dinner. I was really hungry but the plan of eating at a nice restaurant was shot because we had to follow my father's curfew rule for the night. Returning me home late after a very bad start for the night was not going to be acceptable to my parents.

My father, who never said a lot, had much to say upon our late arrival home. He informed my boyfriend that he had been sitting in the living room waiting for my return home at midnight but there had been absolutely no sign of my arrival as my boyfriend had promised. Once the car pulled up and parked for a few minutes I got out and walked toward the house. My father walked out of the front door and met me halfway up the sidewalk and proceeded to inform him that upon our late arrival, he also observed him not opening my car door and escorting me to the front door as a gentleman is required to do for a lady. My very peaceful, loving father who rarely voiced his disappointment of my boyfriend now informed him that he was very disappointed that he had lied about bringing me back on time and not being the gentleman he claimed to be. My father informed him that he was no longer allowed to come to our home again and he did not even want him to physically set a foot in our yard. I knew that my father was very upset but also that he was very forgiving. I simply said good night to both of them and retired to my bedroom for the night.

Even though it had been a very stressful night for me, I found lots of comfort in knowing that I was not the only one who did not have a good time on prom night. I had lots of company in this. I simply decided to feast on the fact that this was my last time experiencing such a night of sheer drama. The greatest irony of this prom night experience is that I didn't even know how to dance. I only knew about shouting and praising the Lord in church; dancing was considered a sin in our church environment because it was the ways of the world. Given the fact that dancing was a major part of prom night activities, I'm absolutely positive that if my parents had realized that piece of information,

I would not have been given permission to attend at all. The activity of dancing at the prom was not on my mind at all, but getting all dressed up and feeling like a King and Queen just as all of my friends would be doing and going out to eat at a nice restaurant afterwards, was certainly on my mind. I wanted to have been able to participate in all of the conversations with my girlfriends after the prom too. I wanted to feel like everybody else.

An example of why I know my parents would not have given me permission to attend the prom had they known dancing was involved is because my older sister had been chosen eight grade class queen while in junior high school, but my parents would not allow her to attend the football game and participate in the activities as queen, such as parading around the football field representing the royal court. I rest my case for those of you readers who may have thought my parents would have said it's ok for me to attend the prom if they had known about the dancing.

But then, the prom nightmare was over and I was preparing to go to college ahead of my classmates. I do not remember my mother saying anything about my boyfriend being late on prom night, but of course, she did not have to say anything. I started preparing to pack for college, forgetting all about the bad habits my boyfriend had displayed. I decided to find happiness in knowing that there would be activities that I would no longer have to complete.

Taking piano lessons was one at the top of my list. I had taken piano lessons every week early in the morning before arriving to my elementary school for the day, starting in the first grade and going all the way to the eleventh grade in high school. My parents would not allow me to quit because they wanted me to always finish what I started. I simply wanted to take piano lessons because my older sister was taking piano lessons and it seemed like lots of fun. I wanted to do what my older sister was doing and my sister wanted to take the lessons because our older aunt, who was only a couple of years older than my sister, was taking them too.

Chapter 3

The Dreaded 12-Inch Wooden Ruler

My piano teacher, a very popular instructor in our community as well as the organist for our senior choir at my church, was preparing all of her music students for the upcoming annual piano recital. She was known for being very strict and would use a 12-inch wooden ruler to hit you on your knuckles if you played the wrong note in the sheet of music you were expected to have already practiced and learned at home before arriving to her home for review. She was a tall black lady with very fair skin and red hair, bleached red similar to Lucille Ball on I Love Lucy with a very loud and deep voice similar to Maud on

The Golden Girls. As you entered the door into her music studio, there would always be other piano students sitting around quietly and nervously waiting for their turn to show how well they had learned their assigned piano lesson for the upcoming recital. My older sister and I would always walk together from home to attend our piano lessons because I was too young for the journey alone.

On this particular morning, as I performed my assigned piano lesson, I struck the wrong note. My piano teacher was sitting in a chair next to me and she immediately hit me very hard on the knuckles with that dreaded 12-inch wooden ruler. I turned my little body around on the piano bench very quickly, looked her dead in her big brown eyes, and shouted at her in my little voice, "THAT HURT MY FINGERS!"

As a child in the third grade in elementary school, shouting at an adult was not an acceptable act in my family. I was so angry for such a little person, but it really did hurt. All of the other piano students got very quiet; my piano teacher looked as though she was in a state of shock! She had never seen me react with such disrespect. I had decided in my young mind that I was tired of her hitting me with that 12-inch wooden ruler and that enough was enough. My piano teacher told me to remove myself from the piano bench and allow my sister to perform her assignment. After my sister completed her piano lesson without incident, we left our teacher's home and walked together to school for the day. On the way to school, my sister told me that she was going to tell our parents about the way I had disrespected our piano teacher. I begged and pleaded with her not to do that, but she said there was nothing I could say or do that would stop her from telling our parents about my disrespectful action towards an adult. I remember going through the day in classes dreading arriving home after school because I knew that as soon as we got there, my sister was going to report my bad behavior from earlier that morning. By the time we got home from school for the day, my piano teacher had already telephoned my mother and reported my behavior earlier that morning. My mother questioned my older sister and of course, she confirmed the incident. I not only received a whipping with a leather belt from my mother, but I also had to apologize in person to my piano teacher for disrespecting her. I really didn't want to apologize because she really did hurt my knuckles, but I did not have a choice in the matter.

In the end, what was fun for my sister and our aunt stopped being fun for me many years after I'd begun piano lessons. The lesson I learned in this situation was, don't do something just because someone else is doing it. But now I was finally free because I was preparing to leave it all behind to attend college!

SWEET INNOCENT NAIVE

Chapter 4

Barbeque Restaurant

Another thing at the top of my list of things I no longer had to do was work in my uncle's barbeque restaurant, which was a promotion from the housework at his and my aunt's home. Once I was old enough to work in the restaurant, the working hours were from 4:00 p.m. to midnight and sometimes later, especially on weekends after a football or basketball game. There were times we would get so busy preparing and serving barbeque sandwiches, rib plates, and other items on the menu for customers that by the end of the night, we would have meat grease all over our aprons. There would be grease on our faces, smoke in our hair, and sometime rude customers who cursed us out for no reason at all.

    While closing at the end of the night one time, we were cleaning the tables and sandwich grills – sweeping and mopping the floors, dissembling the milkshake machine, all with the typical meat grease on our aprons, grease on our faces, and smoke in our hair. We had also restocked to maximum capacity, filling the containers for the sandwiches for the next day's crew. Entering the room with a cigarette hanging out of the side of his mouth came my uncle. He slowly walked up to the cash register, opened the drawer, and pulled out bundles of $20 bills, $10 bills, $5 bills, and $1 dollar bills. Several cash register withdrawals had already been counted and placed in the bank deposit bags earlier during the night. My uncle now placed the bundles of money in his hands, looked at us through his greasy glasses, looked into each of our eyes, and in a very calm, slow, and cold voice, said you all haven't done anything all night long. Puzzled at his comment, we looked at each other and looked back at him and I said to him, you have got to be kidding! Are you out of your mind?! With all the customers' orders we had completed for the night, we were certain we had a successful night. Then he looked at all of us again with the look of sheer disgust on his face before it went away and he smiled.

    Needless to say, he had one of those very dry senses of humor. At times, so dry that you couldn't tell when he was being serious or when he was joking.

Given the late working hours, especially during the week, it was oftentimes difficult getting up for school the next morning, even though there were also lots of times when it was fun working there. Regular customers would come in and we would have lots of fun talking about all kinds of subject and cracking jokes.

There was one very loyal customer: male, approximately 250 pounds, probably 60 years of age, face unshaven, always wearing a dirty red shirt, soiled brown pants, a dirty lime green and white jacket, an old black hat with several holes in the top of the hat pulled down on his head, and dirt-covered dark brown shoes. His personality was very similar to the character of Otis Campbell on The Andy Griffith Show. This one particular customer would always order just one black cup of piping hot coffee. Also, very much like Otis Campbell, he was always plastered, harmless to others, and would always make his grand entrance through the doors of the restaurant to the counter. Barely standing up at the counter mumbling his order of one cup of coffee please with his raspy voice, he would stagger away to sit in a booth with a table for four, mumbling to himself words that we could not understand. Once he had received his hot cup of coffee, he would attempt to lift the container of sugar with his uncontrollably shaking hands and try to pour some sugar into his piping-hot cup of black coffee. In the past, we'd tried to assist him, but we all quickly learned that he never wanted any assistance. Therefore, at the end of his visit with us, there would always be more sugar on the table than in his piping hot cup of coffee. Sometimes he would try to have a conversation with my uncle, but the only words we could ever understand was when he would call my uncle's first name, and my uncle would simply nod his head in response. After saying my uncle's name, though, there was only the sound of someone mumbling with their lips partially closed together. We could never understand this customer's long-winded words, when he was moving his lips mumbling to himself and to us, but we all knew based on his history, that he just wanted to order a cup of black piping hot coffee. To be respectful to him, we never allowed him to see us hysterically laughing because he could never seem to pour the sugar into his cup of coffee. Most of the time he missed the cup, and white sugar spilled all over the table due to his physical state. He would lift up the cup of coffee with his shaking hands, sip coffee from the hot cup a few times, mumble something in a very raspy voice for a while, and begin laughing for a moment before he would attempt to work his way out of the booth from the table and stagger out of the door the same way he entered. During all of his visits with us, he never bothered other customers sitting in the booths. Similar to Otis Campbell on The Andy Griffith Show, many of our customers knew of him or knew some members of his family and knew that he was harmless. It was always fun when he staggered in the doors of the restaurant, even though there was very little verbal communication between him and us. He never knew that he made the nights he entered, fun for all of us.

Working at my uncle's restaurant as a teenager taught me a lot about how to deal with the public and how to serve others, and I developed good work habits and ethics. My parents taught us how to be responsible and how to save the money we earned as well as how to purchase little items for ourselves.

My uncle always wore a softball type cap and a blue or gray jumpsuit. A cigarette would be hanging out of the side of his mouth while he was talking, and his eyeglass lenses were always dirty from grease & smoke from the preparation of the meat in the barbeque smoke pit. The lenses of his eyeglass were so dirty that I never understood how he could see out of them clearly, until one day I asked him about it. How did he manage when his eyeglasses were so dirty that the lenses were grey? I even offered to clean them for him. But he told me that the mess on his lenses kept him from seeing things that he probably did not want to see anyway, so he liked them just the way they were: dirty.

My uncle was a good-hearted person, with lots of wisdom and to my knowledge, never went to church but he would give you a sermonette if you asked him a question on just about anything. He had his own opinion about all subjects and according to him, he was correct most of the time – unless you could prove him incorrect. Customers of all ethnic groups and all walks of life would come into the restaurant, not just for the food but also to listen to his opinions about life in general. He always had an opinion about every subject. I'm not sure where he got his opinions from because he was not a world traveler who had been exposed to different kinds of cultures or environments, but he was always sure about what he would tell you. Also, he would always say something that the average person would have never thought about. My aunt could discern negative spirits in people she met like the back of her hand; they were both good people and very hard workers. I enjoyed being around them both as well as working with my oldest sister, my brother, and a couple of my cousins and friends who were also employees. We all grew up together working in my uncle's restaurant. Because of our age, it was a first-time job for many of us and other young people of other ethnic groups within our community.

But after a while, I began to hate coming home after school and receiving a telephone call either before I would arrive home or shortly after arriving, saying that I would be needed to replace someone who was not able to come to work. I looked forward to enjoying coming home from school like many of my classmates who were not working and not feeling so tense due to the possibility of that dreaded telephone call.

But I was now free from many things that I no longer

enjoyed doing. For me, there would be no more early morning piano lessons, no more of the dreaded 12-inch wooden ruler on my knuckles, and also no more long afternoon-to-midnight restaurant shifts working after a day at school. I could have shouted from the highest mountaintop in a loud voice: "I'm Free!"

I decided to focus on my future, my new adventure of being in college, and the chance of making new friends. I was ready to say goodbye to my family, friends, and the drama with my boyfriend, even though I still loved him in my heart. I had not given up on him yet.

SWEET INNOCENT NAIVE

Chapter 5

Leaving For College

My parents packed the car and took me to college for a new life adventure. When I left home for college, I had in mind the goal of becoming a research scientist because at that time I loved science. I could just visualize myself walking around in one of those white coats in a research lab like I'd seen on TV.

My sister was a senior at the same college. Upon my arrival on the first day of college as freshmen, the first requirement I was scheduled to complete was to attend the New Freshmen Orientation, which of course I did not attend. According to my sister and her friends, my next task was to throw away that ugly blue and white stripe

New Freshmen beanie cap, made similar to a navy sailor's cap, that I was required to wear on campus signifying the status of new freshmen. I was delighted to throw that ugly cap away because I was going to be hanging out with my sister and her friends who were all college seniors and in my young mind, everyone would think that I was also a senior in college.

Wow! What a first day! We were an all-girl private school with young ladies from all around the world; there were lots of rules and regulations to be followed and lots of new cultural exposure in store to be experienced. One of the girls in my sister's group had a Cadillac on campus that her boyfriend allowed her to use when needed. It was nothing for us to go out to eat at a nice restaurant and enjoy a good steak. I was the baby of the group and these were all seniors and friends of my sister, so I never had to pay for anything. WOW! I must admit, they all spoiled me with anything I wanted! The mother of one of the girls in the group would call to check on her daughter but she would always ask her "are you all taking care of the baby?"

After the first year of classes in biology, chemistry, and zoology, I quickly changed my mind about my planned major in biology. One of my professors in chemistry talked very fast, and as he lectured, he would write on the chalkboard at the same time. While we were trying to listen to what he was saying and write down the notes he was writing on the chalkboard, he would erase the written notes he'd already completed and begin writing new ones. It was very difficult and frustrating to keep up with his style of teaching.

Since I had always sung in the church choir at home, I started participating in the college choir, the college concert choir, the gospel choir, and the gospel quartet. Because the college choir and college quartet represented the college, there was a lot of traveling involved. The college quartet included me, my sister, and two other seniors who were my sisters' best friends, but they named me the baby of the group because I was the youngest. Even today, after almost forty years, they still call me "the baby." As the college singing quartet, we completed special traveling assignments in Montgomery, AL; Chicago, IL; Atlanta, GA; and other states, sometimes with the president of our college and other college officials, and sometime alone representing the college with all-expenses-paid trips. This was the experience of a lifetime for someone so young. I was already ahead of my friends left in my small Southern hometown. While they were still trying to graduate from high school, some of them wondering if they would graduate at all and if so what college they would attend, I was already in college, hanging out with seniors, traveling, and singing representing my college. This was the Life!

The music department produced a play during my first year there and I decided to participate, just as something to do that could be fun. The play and my participation were such a success that the chairman of the music department insisted I change my major from biology to music because of the type of voice she recognized I had. This was an easy decision for me because my classes included biology, zoology, and chemistry, which were all about to kick my buttocks at the same time. The picture of seeing myself wearing a white research coat in a research lab, completing intense research projects, quickly vanished. Singing seemed to have come to me very easily because it was something that I had done all of my life, being a preacher's kid and always in church choirs. I was too immature to understand the fact that singing was really a gift from God and that He was simply using me as one of His vessels to sing through. That angelic voice was His voice and not mine. This is a lesson many of us miss – that no matter what, our gifts and talents are due to our levels of immaturity in life and in the things of God.

We can never take credit for what God chooses to do through us. Always try to remember that it's God and not you. Our job is to yield to God and let Him use us because He will not force Himself on us, but He will go to someone else who is willing to be used by Him. He's looking for a clean vessel to work through; therefore, we must have clean hands and a pure heart. Remember, none of us are perfect, but we should be striving for perfection until Jesus returns.

Chapter 6

A Life-Changing Experience

The mental thought of not having biology, chemistry, and zoology classes were a welcomed change in my mind and therefore, like many immature young people, I took the easy way out. I changed my major to music, with a concentration in vocal music. It had been determined by the chairman of the music department that I had the voice of a lyric soprano, which was described as being like an opera singer: having a light voice and a melodic style. As a vocal music major, I was expected to study French, German, and Italian because the songs that I had to sing as a vocal music major would be in these languages. I later received a music scholarship via the chairman of the music department to study opera in Graz, Austria for the summer via a program called the American Institute of Musical Studies (AIMS). The curriculum involved singers doing extensive work in vocal technique, diction, psychological, musical and dramatic preparation for performing and auditioning, body movement, literary and historical studies, and the stagecraft to present their repertoire. The AIMS approach fosters a professional attitude toward the art, craft, and business of vocal music throughout the program. Participants are exposed directly to the practices and competitiveness of the music world. Opera studio participants worked closely with European and American opera coaches, conductors, and stage directors. Concentration is on the standard operatic repertoire (German, Italian, and French) with emphasis on the works of Mozart and Strauss.

This summer program would last for six weeks, and of course my grandmother was, like many toward her grandchild leaving the country for the very first time and such a young age, very protective of me. My grandmother, who had never traveled outside of the US, informed me that I should not go because something might happen, like war could break out! My parents simply ignored my grandmother's fears and were all for this great opportunity for their daughter. My sister made arrangements for all of my required documents, packed my bags, and made sure I had extra personal spending money from my family. Then I was ready to leave and meet other music students who had also received musical scholarships from their institutions all across the United States.

As young as I was, I did not have any fear of meeting other people; I think that being a preacher's kid, traveling from city to city with my parents and grandparents, actually prepared me for such an experience. I was accustomed to meeting people, so that was not new for me. I can say without a doubt that I was beyond excited looking forward to going to a different country with a different culture, one that I would have probably never even dreamed about. I was in sheer disbelief that this opportunity had been granted to me. I remember saying to myself, I'm the new kid in the music department and there were others that they could have given the scholarship to, so why me? I also remember thinking to myself, who do they think I am that they would give this opportunity to me? I can only conclude that, once again, God had granted me favor, placing me ahead of the class.

All of the students for the special AIMS program met as a group in New York City at the LaGuardia Airport. We were informed as a group that some students were music students and others were geography students headed to a different destination than the music students. Everyone and their bags were checked in, and our airplane with over 200 students left at midnight for Europe. What an experience of a lifetime for a sixteen-year-old black girl from a small Southern town! My sister made sure that my parents understood that this was an opportunity of a lifetime. They made financial as well as physical sacrifices to make sure I received everything required for this opportunity. My parents and sister never said, we do not think you should go because they did not have any money; instead, funds were created for my personal expenses. The trip's requirements included the need for an evening gown that was required for one night's attendance at the opera in Vienna. My mother, an expert seamstress, made sure I had a beautiful white chiffon floor-length gown trimmed with sequins, with a matching white jacket and attached hood trimmed with white feathers, matching sandal shoes, clutch purse, and teardrop style earrings to complete the ensemble for a night at the opera in Vienna. My parents and sister never displayed either a look or a word of "you should not go." They recognized this as the opportunity of a lifetime, and they encouraged me to go forward and learn everything I could as well as have a great time. They were my backbone during a time in my life when I would not have known what decision to make with such an opportunity. I was very young, and it was a major decision to make for someone who was only sixteen years old. What did I know?

 A word to all parents: allow your child to experience such chances of a lifetime by encouraging them to go forward in whatever they are doing as long as it's nothing that will harm them or others. Let them have a chance of a lifetime experience. Another word of advice, though: have someone you trust do the research on what your child want to do first and never let a child make an adult decision.

SWEET INNOCENT NAIVE

Chapter 7

Graz, Austria

Austria is home to spectacular cities and towns, majestic mountain peaks, pristine alpine lakes, a rich and storied history, and enticing dining scene, just to mention a few of some of the things that make travel there so amazing. Found in the heart of Europe, the country of Austria borders Germany, Switzerland, the Czech Republic, Slovakia, Hungary, Italy, and Slovenia. The second largest city in Austria after Vienna, Graz is an ideal blend of old and new. Found in southeastern Austria, Graz is over 850 years old and the capital of the Austrian province of Steiermark (Styria). Its beautifully restored Old City, the largest in Europe, is an architectural treasure and is rated by National Geographic as the fifth most recommended destination in the world. The rich cultural tradition of Graz and Steiermark dates to the 14th century when Graz was the residence of the Austrian Emperor.

As a little sixteen-year-old, 5'0", 90-pound, black girl from the southern US, I boarded a flight out of North Carolina for the flight that was expected to leave at midnight out of New York City's LaGuardia Airport with AIMS officials and over 200 students as passengers. Our airplane for this traveling adventure was a Boeing 747, scheduled to arrive in Graz, Austria by noon the next day. I had traveled via airplane before while visiting my family at home for the holidays, but I had never been on an airplane this large. For a 16-year-old, this plane was very, very large! I could not believe the number of people traveling on one airplane! There were long rows of seats in the middle aisle, long rows on each side of the middle aisle, and a spiral staircase leading up to an upper level. I was simply amazed! The airplane was filled with an atmosphere of suspense and excitement. I did not have any idea what to expect in reference to where I was traveling. Based on my observations, I knew that I was not the only student feeling a level of excitement, anxiousness, suspense, numbness, and at the same time, somewhat in a state of shock. This was really happening to me! I was not dreaming! All through the night I tossed and turned in my seat with a blanket around my shoulders, shivering because it was a little cold on the airplane. In my mind too, I was trying to anticipate what was going to happen upon our arrival in Austria and at the same time I was attempting to portray a degree of calmness. I could not seem to get warm, so I finally asked the stewardess for an additional blanket and a pillow. When I received them, I took a deep breath and finally settled down in my spirit, falling asleep with a soft pillow underneath my head and blankets around my shoulders.

As I opened my eyes the next morning, I looked out of the airplane window and saw the beautiful golden sunlight shining through, and a perfect light blue sky as others began to awaken. As I looked around at the other students, I pinched myself in sheer disbelief that this adventure was really happening to me and I was not just dreaming! The stewardess began serving our breakfast trays for the morning, which consisted of eggs, toast, bacon, and orange juice, which was perfect to keep us from being hungry until lunch.

It was a very long flight to Austria and we were just about ready for landing that morning when the stewardess announced, fasten your seatbelts. The captain began his standard end-of-the-flight speech to us over the loudspeaker preparing for the landing process when all of a sudden he yelled out a couple of choice words and the airplane suddenly jerked upward, ascending in high-speed motion as several people screamed. Soon afterward, the airplane began descending again and leveled off as the stewardess attempted to calm several passengers. We began looking at each wondering what was happening and just at that moment, we were informed by the captain over the loudspeaker that he had been given the green light for landing by the airport tower when suddenly out of the blue, another large airplane was in our path. The captain explained that in order to avoid a head-on collision with the other airplane, he had had no choice but to ascend our airplane to a higher altitude, and he apologized for the fear the incident had caused. Everyone clapped and cheered for our captain's piloting skills. As we began departing from the airplane, we thanked him for his quick thinking that had saved our lives.

Organized in smaller groups departing the airplane, we were escorted by our U.S. officials of the AIMS organization out of the airport, along with all of our luggage, and loaded on to buses. As the buses drove away from the airport, I remember looking out of the window of the bus and seeing beautiful green mountain tops, vibrantly colored flowers, and a very peaceful atmosphere. I also noticed that the streets seemed to be unusually clean to me. We traveled several miles through the city and the bus finally pulled up to a two-story red brick that would be our dormitory for the summer with two girls per room. Imagine being the sweet, innocent, and naïve southern black sixteen-year-old with over 200 Caucasian students from different parts of the U.S. I was not prejudiced, in fact one of my best friends in my southern hometown was Caucasian. My experience working in my uncle's restaurant enhanced my ability to adjust to all types of people. Therefore, this was not a new experience for me and I was very comfortable with the roommate assignment.

There were four of us young ladies who hung out together during this experience in Austria because our rooms were near each other. The rooms were small, but nice enough for two people. It was my first experience sleeping under a white goose down comforter. It was soft and warm during the cool nights; I could feel the soft feathers all throughout the comforter. Imagine holding soft white clouds around your body all night long – it was simply wonderful! Because I never forgot that comforter experience at such a young age, as an adult I purchased two white goose down comforters. What a lasting impression that made upon me.

A couple of the girls were instrumental musicians; one of them played the trumpet, the other a guitar, and the third girl was a voice major like me. Each day at the dormitory, we shared breakfast, lunch, and dinner together. I enjoyed a particular soup that we students had named "Brain Soup," which looked much like tiny dark brown balls in dark brown liquid. It did not look very appetizing or inviting, but it had a very good taste. After I adjusted to the name and the look of it, I was able to eat this soup with a sandwich. But there was another famous dish that was served daily by the name of "Tongue Soup" that I simply could not eat and did not eat. It literally consisted of a cow's tongue with the taste buds! No way was this little Southern black girl going to eat that!

Soups are popular when it comes to Austria dining, and among the country's favorites are Gulyassuppe and Leberknodlsuppe. The former is a kind of Hungarian goulash; it is a savory stew of beef that is spiced with paprika. Pork is also used in goulashes, while the latter is comprised of chicken liver-stuffed dumplings and a meaty broth. In Salzburg, the most renowned dessert specialty is called Salzburger Nockerlin, which is a type of meringue pie, and because of its creamy peaks, it is said to resemble the Alps that dominate the nearby countryside.

In Vienna, Wiener Schnitzel, which is breaded and fried veal, is for all intents and purposes a national dish. Wiener Schnitzel was my absolute favorite choice of meat!

My new friends and I took classes related to our areas of concentration, such as individual voice lessons, stage artistry, German, French, Italian and English diction classes, and Master Classes; also, we all encouraged each other during this musical and life-changing experience. The four of us went on guided tours of Austria together, which included tours in Salzburg, the birthplace of Wolfgang Amadeus Mozart, founded in the heart of town called Mozart's Geburtshaus. This was a multi-story yellow building with white shutters. Three of the floors have been turned into a museum. Mozart's images are found all over the city of Salzburg. I simply could not believe I was seeing the setting of the Oscar-winning film The Sound of Music graced by Julie Andrews dancing and singing on the hill in 1965. We toured the 17th century Mirabell Palace, which was known for its immaculate gardens, and the Petersfriedhof, or St. Peter's Cemetery, which is regarded as one of the most charming cemeteries in the world with many of Salzburg's past aristocratic families buried there including Mozart's sister Nannerl. Salzburg Cathedral, or Salzburg Dom, a 17th century baroque masterpiece where Mozart was baptized, was another stop in our journeys. Imagine looking through the eyes of a sixteen-year-old as I saw the Schonbrum Palace Vienna (modeled after the Palace of Versailles in France) with its 1,441 rooms, many employing the elaborate and ornamental Rococo style employed including the Room of Millions, which was undeniably ornate with gold-trimmed doors, beautiful paintings, and exquisite 18th century furniture. Large crystal_chandeliers hung over long dining room tables for large dinner parties. Even the gardens at Schonbrum Palace were meticulous and dazzling. I had never seen such large rooms, gold-trimmed doors, gold-trimmed furniture, and large crystal chandeliers in my life. Can you imagine being in the Schonbrum Palace? In my opinion, not even the Biltmore house in Asheville, North Carolina, as grand as it is, could be compared to the European palaces that

I toured as a sixteen-year-old. In Salzburg, we toured Hohensalzburg Fortress, which looms over the city from its perch on Festungsberg Hill; it is easily seen from most, if not all, vantage points in the city. Hohensalzburg Fortress is the largest preserved fortress in all of central Europe. In the middle of Old Town Vienna is Hofburg Palace, where the Vienna Boys' Choir performs, and you can catch the impressive horse show at the Spanish Riding School. In Vienna, we also toured the St. Stephens Cathedral, which is a spectacular Romanesque and Gothic style church, the most important religious building in the city.

Chapter 8

German Street Car Experience

One day while my friends and I were riding on the streetcar in Graz sightseeing from one destination to another, a precious little German girl around the age of six approached me. Her skin was olive in tone, and she had the most beautiful quarter-sized dark brown eyes I had ever seen. She had beautiful long brown hair parted in the middle, combed into two braids with a blue ribbon at the end of each braid, and she was wearing an electric blue-and-white-striped dress. This little girl stood right in front of me, just staring at me while I was enjoying the sights. At first, I simply ignored her stare, but since she was not leaving, I looked over and smiled at her before continuing to view the sights. One of my friends looked at me as if to say, what's her problem? But I didn't know.

Then the little girl started moving closer to me, taking one of her tiny little hands and rubbing the right side of my cheek. I smiled at her again while her mother attempted to remove her hand to stop her from stroking my cheek. Her mother began to apologize to me for her daughter's behavior, but I assured her mother that it was fine and I allowed the little girl to continue stroking my cheek, but this time, both of my cheeks with both of her tiny little hands. I'd remembered being informed in one of our orientation sessions upon our arrival that the German people in this area were not accustomed to seeing very many black people, and therefore, I felt this was a new experience for the little girl. I felt honored to have made such a contribution to this little German girl's experience. We were just about to arrive at our next destination when her mother thanked me, with what little English she could speak, for allowing her daughter to have such a precious experience.

My friends and I departed from the streetcar and began touring the streets of downtown Graz together. We purchased wonderful breads and cheeses that I had never eaten before. Shopping was my favorite thing to do, and it was the season of the year in Graz when merchants would have seventy-five percent or more sales off the regular price of items in all of the stores, and I took full advantage of these sales. I had to request more money from home because I had not learned to really budget and be as good a steward of money as I thought. Of course, my family wired more personal spending money to me because they wanted me to enjoy this experience. I mailed lots of purchased items such as designer coats, suits, dresses and shoes, back to North Carolina to my sister for safekeeping. It also eliminated the need for extra baggage upon my journey back to the United States. My friends and I also took lots of pictures to share with our families and friends at college and at home.

SWEET INNOCENT NAIVE

Chapter 9

Day In The Sun

Since my friends were all Caucasian women, they decided that it was time to put on our bathing suits and enjoy a little swimming and sun tanning. This particular day that we decided to go was the day of my 17th birthday. After our classes ended for the day, we all put on our bathing suits and sat by the pool, suntanning. While we were having a good time chatting about our experiences in Austria, our classes, the sights, and my birthday, a very handsome man approached us. He was about 6′ 0″ with silky straight shoulder-length honey-blond hair and the most gorgeous light blue eyes that looked like the clear blue sky, as well as beautiful straight pearly-white teeth with an awesome dark olive tan. He asked where we were from and we informed him that we were from the United States. He shared with us, in a very soft and dreamy tone of voice, that he was Swedish. As he talked, he kept staring at me and then he asked me, how did I get such a beautiful tan! I politely informed him that I had been sun tanning "all day long." Of course, he was simply amazed that I could get such a tan in just a day. He told me how beautiful I was and of course I replied very proudly with a "thank you." When he left, the four of us had a great time laughing. A couple of the girls laughed so hard they fell out of their lounge chairs because he did not seem to know that I was really a beautiful seventeen-year-old black girl parading around in a white bathing suit and white sun glasses, not a beautiful white girl with a great tan.

Because it was my birthday, while we were sitting around the pool tanning and making plans for later that afternoon to celebrate my birthday, someone came to the poolside to inform me that I had received a telephone call. I jumped out of my lounge chair and ran to the lobby. When I picked up the telephone and said hello, it was my family members on the other end calling to wish me a Happy Birthday! I was truly surprised to hear from them. That really made my day perfect!

But no, I did not hear from my hometown boyfriend on this very special day in my life. I had decided that maybe he could not afford the telephone call, especially when I later learned that the call was $23 per min. I gave him this excuse for not calling. But in my heart, I was still a little disappointed that he did not make any effort since I was out of the country. I made an effort to hide my disappointment from my new friends because we were having such a wonderful time, and I did not want anything to change our fun at the pool.

Later that night, because it was my birthday, my friends took me out to a restaurant to celebrate. I ordered my favorite meat, Wiener Schnitzel, along with potatoes, salad, and soda pop. We laughed a lot and had so much fun that one would have thought we were drinking, but we were not. The photos we took that night made it look as though we were plastered. One of the girls had her head leaning back with a bottle in her hand and her eyes were staring to the top of the room, and our eyes looked red due to the glare from the flash of the camera. We were drinking but only bottles of soda pop and acting as though we were drunk. We were all church girls, plus I was the daughter and granddaughter of preachers, so even this many miles away from home, I had the fear of God within me – or maybe just, at that age, the fear of my parents. That was the result of good home training and a life of church doctrine and ethics. People generally say that the preacher's kids go wild once they leave home and go to college, but I was not one of the wild preacher's kids that so many people have stereotyped.

SWEET INNOCENT NAIVE

Chapter 10

Opera In Vienna

Our group of music students arrived in Austria during the peak season of the famous Austrian Opera Festival in Vienna, with all expenses paid! We would travel approximately two hours from Graz to Vienna for the music Opera Festival. Our orientation materials had made us aware of the proper attire to pack for the different events that we would attend during the summer.

It was now time to get all dressed up in our long beautiful and colorful evening gowns to attend the opera. One of the girls wore a lovely mint green gown, another wore a soft yellow gown, and the other wore a beautiful bright powder blue gown. I wore a beautiful long flowing white gown, with a shawl trimmed with silver that my mother had designed for me to wear to the opera. We were very excited because this was going to be the first time in our lives ever attending the opera and we also just happened to be in Vienna, Austria. WOW!

We arrived in the front of the building and departed the vehicle to the steps of the opera house in Vienna where women were elegantly dressed in their long evening gowns of all colors, large diamond rings, diamond necklaces, and earrings with mink stoles draped around their shoulders because of the coolness of the night. Most of them were also escorted by men dressed in black tuxedos. This scene was simply beyond my wildest dreams! What an awesome experience to witness all of this grandeur at such a young age!

As we walked in the lobby through the main doors, the atmosphere was filled with the air of elegance and wealth. Couples were seated in the private booths with opera glasses in their hands, taking in the view of the people moving about in the auditorium preparing to be seated before the start of the opera. This was just as I had seen in many classic American movies, and I had always imagined myself being a participant of such awesome event. As the curtains opened, the orchestra began to play. The Opera La Traviata was performed by professional opera singers EXQUISITELY dressed for the opera being performed. It was absolutely divine! I felt as though I was dreaming and unable to wake up! I was in a state of shock to be in that environment and sitting in the audience with people who seemed to simply project the sheer spirit of wealth, elegance, and an atmosphere of classical music intellects. Imagine being someone who spent most of her time in church and had only seen such an event in the old movies replaying on television.

As parents, no matter what the area of your children's interest, please make every possible effort and allow them to have such an experience if the opportunity should ever come. It will be the experience of a lifetime, and one they will never forget!

SWEET INNOCENT NAIVE

Chapter 11

Defeating The Challenge

Back in Graz after the opera, my schedule of classes gave me the opportunity to sing before a world-renowned conductor, who sometimes served as an instructor in the master classes for vocal music students. He was a German man approximately 60 years or older with a thin white head of hair, a very harsh and grumpy voice, piercing light blue eyes that seem to look straight through you, and a no-nonsense personality. His facial features were similar to the news personality Andy Rooney on *60 Minutes*; he was also very curt, the epitome of an "Intimidator" personality.

At that time, I did not know what to call his spirit that was so powerful in the room. I just knew that I and many of the other vocal students were simply terrified of singing in front of him. I had not experienced such a strong personality before, and I could not imagine how I was going to get through this challenge.

One day in our vocal master class, a young lady was singing before him and suddenly he very rudely told her to please stop singing because according to him, listening to her voice was similar to hearing someone using their fingers scratching the surface of a chalk board. He informed her in front of the entire class that, in his opinion, she should never sing another note. He was so brutal and disgusted with her that he advised her to change her career. The young lady looked at him as though she was in a state of shock, then ran down the side steps of the stage and out of the main doors of the room crying because he had been so critical of her singing in front of the entire master classroom. Needless to say, she was totally embarrassed and hurt. It was as though she had been hit by a freight train, but with words. The tension in the room was so thick, you could cut it with a knife. Everyone was very quiet and hesitant of being the next student to sing on center stage. Intense fear gripped my heart at that very moment, but I made up my mind that I would not be intimidated by him. The instructor was so disgusted that he ended the Master Class session for the rest of the day. We were all delighted that he had ended the session for the day, and everyone quietly got up out of our chairs and left the room.

As vocal music students, we were given assigned dates that we were scheduled to perform in front of this instructor. Based on my schedule, I had about one week to prepare; therefore, I made a promise to myself that I would be ready. This meant lots of intense practicing with my vocal coach on the music given to me and lots of praying on my part.

During the vocal master classes, I believed that the other students were excellent singers, but after their performances, this world-renowned instructor concluded that they were not. Of course, I was totally confused by his decisions, but now that I have matured, I understand that I was too young and inexperienced, both musically and professionally, to really evaluate what was good or bad singing. As for myself, I was determined to meet the challenge of taking the brutal criticism from this instructor. I was the only minority student in the room, and I was not going to allow him to make me cry in front of all the other students. Even if I wanted to cry afterwards, I was determined not to cry right there, no matter how brutal the instructor was. I was going to wait until I returned to my room in the dormitory and have a private cry there if necessary.

All of us were stressing out because of this instructor, who gave such brutal and critical evaluations after so many of the student performances. We were stressing out, finally realizing that these classes were not just for fun, but we were all expected to pass the classes we were registered to complete for the summer. We were in Austria to study and our grades would be transferred to our official college records at our respective colleges and universities. This was not just a trip to Europe for having fun, but also a trip for learning more about how to sing or play using the gifts God had blessed all of us with. Mediocre performances were not acceptable.

After realizing this, each day I spent lots of time in the private practice music rooms for singers, at times with my personal vocal coach as well as during my time alone, with intense grilling on learning the German language, memorizing the words of the song, and improving my diction, musical pitch, and stage presence. I had made up my mind that I was not going to give this instructor the satisfaction of making me cry and embarrassing me in front of all the other students as he had done with many others. Additionally, given the fact that I was the only black student in the room, the pressure was really on. An intense level of personal pride and determination had kicked in.

After several days of waiting and listening to others sing had passed, now it was my turn to sing in front of this highly critical and world-renowned vocal music instructor. As we all entered the master classroom and took our seats, the instructor reached for the roster and my name was called as the first performer to sing. I remember saying to myself, oh no, because I hated being first, but then I took a deep breath and slowly rose though my body did not want to move; I went forward from my seat one step at a time. As I walked towards the front of the classroom, I could feel the tension begin rising in the room. I looked at several of the students as I passed them, and they all had a look of doom and gloom on their faces. I placed my hand over my heart and felt it beating seemingly faster than normal. But I slowly put one foot forward at a time as I walked up the side steps to the center area of the stage. I felt as though my knees were going to buckle and give out on me. I began feeling afraid that when the music started, I was not going to be able to sing the first note of the song I had spent so much time intensely preparing with my assigned vocal coach, making sure the accuracy of the German pronunciation and musical pitch was sharp and not flat.

    I finally reached center stage, though, and turned to the audience of fellow students and that intimidating vocal master class instructor. I quietly cleared my throat and placed one foot slightly before the other as we were trained to do in our Stage Preparation Class as being the posed standing position of a professional singer. The spotlight was directed on center stage, shining on me as though I was an opera star singing on stage, with the intimidator and the students being my audience. I focused my eyes straight ahead, but slightly over the heads of the students and the intimidator instead of direct eye contact, as we were trained to do. This was a mechanism used to help singers not become nervous and distracted when performing before an audience.

There were lots of thoughts in those few seconds running through my mind such as: *I wish this was already over, I wish I did not have to do this* and *what have I gotten myself into？ I wish this* and *I wish that* and feeling like I was going to pass out. Finally, I got ahold of myself and decided within my heart and mind to simply forget about the instructor and the other students who were in room. With my mind made up, I nodded my head slightly to say that I was ready and the music started. Then when I opened my mouth to sing, the first note was a perfect pitch! When I heard that clear and perfect pitch, I simply continued singing my heart out until the end of the song. Once I reached the end, I was so happy to be finished that I really did not care what the intimidators' comments would be, because it was over! I was also thrilled to have finished without passing out on the floor!

To my surprise and sheer shock, the vocal instructor "intimidator" was very complimentary of my singing ability. This brutal and highly critical instructor informed me that I had sung the aria with perfect pitch, excellent pronunciation of the German language, excellent interpretation of the music, and excellent stage presence. He also said that I had a very beautiful lyric soprano voice and with diligence and hard work, I could do very well in a career of opera. I had defeated the challenge! After having somewhat of a good experience mixed with fear, pride, and determination, I began thinking to myself, maybe singing opera really was the route for me to take for my future career.

Later though, while feeling good about the possibility of a career in opera, I observed adult men and women running all over the place after class in the dormitory; some appeared to be very drunk, and most were loud and cursing. Based on that observation I resolved maybe it was not something for a sheltered, Christian, and just-turning-seventeen young black girl to see, because that scene was a real turn-off for me. I did not like what I was seeing and hearing, because I was accustomed to a more structured or organized environment. As a_result, I decided to just focus on my studies and do the very best I could with all of my classes, which included studying German, French, and Italian, diction classes, stage artistry, individual vocal lessons, aria coaching, vocal master classes, and daily conversational German for musicians.

Even though I was able to master the challenges of my classes, I was informed that I not only had a beautiful voice but also that I would need to gain a couple of hundred pounds in order to be able to properly vocally project as an opera singer. Also, music would have to be my number one priority in my life, and nothing and no one could be more important to me than singing opera. At that time,

I weighed only 90 pounds and I was not about to gain more weight just to sing opera. Furthermore, someday I wanted to have a family with the boyfriend I had left in my hometown. Based on the requirements given to me for a career in opera, I'd decided within my mind, that no, this opera business was really not the direction for me. It was not that important that I would make such sacrifices in my life. My inner thoughts were, no way!

A word of advice again to all parents: never let a child make an adult decision. What did I really know at age seventeen? Now that I think about it, absolutely nothing.

My new friends and I successfully completed our classes, and then the summer program was ending, and it was time for all of us to return to the US to our respective colleges and universities. It was difficult saying goodbye to these three new friends I had shared such an awesome experience with. We had been learning about a new culture, encouraging each other to meet the challenges each of us had endured during our classroom experiences, and learning about each other for three months in Europe. We all made promises that we would keep in touch and we did for a while until we all grew older and simply lost contact with each other.

Chapter 12

Life After The Graz, Austria Adventure

I returned to my college campus after completing the summer program in Graz, Austria with my mind well made up that a career in opera was really not for me. It was good to know that a world-renowned conductor in Europe thought that I had great vocal abilities, and a great potential to do very well in the opera arena, but number one, I was not going to gain more weight. I was 90 pounds and I liked being at that weight. Number two, I was not going to have singing opera be my lifetime priority, because nothing was going to be more important to me than getting married and having two kids (a boy and a girl, preferably in that order) with my one and only love-of-my-life boyfriend since the tenth grade, who I had left in my small Southern hometown.

No way was I going to devote myself entirely to opera! And I mean *no way*!

Once I returned to my college campus, I had a meeting with the chairwoman of the music department. She had decided that due to my experience and the maturity of my voice and abilities, it was clear that I needed a more challenging voice instructor than the ones who were available on my campus. In her words, I needed someone who would challenge me and bring out the very best that God had placed in me.

So, this chairwoman of my college's music department conducted a search at several of the local universities in the city and finally felt that she had located the perfect private voice instructor for me. I would travel across the city at the expense of my institution to complete private vocal lessons from this challenging new voice instructor who would be perfect for me, according to the chairwoman of my music department. Of course, I never informed her that I no longer had such a strong interest in opera. I decided, since I enjoyed music and it seemed easy to me, that I would complete the process of getting a degree in music. In my inner thoughts, though, I did not have any plans of doing anything with a music degree upon graduation. For one thing, I was very sure that I most certainly did not want to teach music at any educational level or on any pay scale.

After several weeks of the chairwoman of my music

department searching for a new and a more challenging voice instructor for me, the task was finally completed. I received a called to finally meet the new voice instructor at the office of his institution, so I traveled to his campus and located his office, where the secretary invited me to have a seat in one of the chairs. As I looked around, I noticed all types of music awards and professional certificates hanging on the wall and around on his desk. Then the office door opened as he walked in and I turned around in my seat. To my shock as I looked up, he was a very tall and lanky white man smoking a long pipe!!! Even though I'm not prejudiced, I said to myself, this is really going to be a real change for me. To have gone from an easy-going short black female voice instructor to a tall white man who smoked a pipe! His height was intimidating enough even before the fact that he smoked a pipe, but I could not tolerate smoking in my presence, even from my friends. I remember thinking "I'm not sure how this is going to work out, but I'll give it a try." I guess God was still teaching me to accept people as they are, not as I would have them to be.

This new voice instructor invited me to sit in the chair in front of his long office desk and then the telephone rang. As I looked around his office while he took the telephone call, I could see bookshelves full of musical books, sheet music on a nearby table, and a piano on the other side of the room. I remember thinking to myself, what have

I gotten myself into? He finally ended his telephone conversation with the pipe still hanging out of his mouth as he apologized for the interruption. We began talking a little about myself and my family's background as well as his background to break the ice. Because of his obvious level of maturity, I'm sure he could sense that I was a little hesitant. He discussed his plans and goals for me as one of his private voice students, explaining that he had been informed of my needs by the chairwoman of my music department. He told me that he would make every effort to accomplish those needs, but it was going to be hard work on the part of the both of us. The music he had selected for me to sing was going to be very challenging. I would be expected to memorize each song and they would be in French, German, and Italian as well as English.

I remember now beginning to feel some of the same emotions that I had felt when I had to perform in the presence of the world-renowned conductor voice instructor from that master class in Graz, Austria – the one with the "intimidator" personality. My new private voice instructor was similar in personality, I thought. OH NO!!!

After getting past the initial shock of the intimidating personality that I had been challenged with before, the work began with my diction and not singing. The first word was learning how to pronounce the word "asked." With my southern vernacular, I had a habit of pronouncing the word as "axed." He kept saying the two words but I could not hear the difference between them until he showed me by demonstrating what happens when you say the word axe. His example was a person taking the "axe" and chopping a piece of wood. That picture became very clear to me and I never said the word "axed" for the word "asked" again. We had just experienced a major breakthrough with the language barrier! It was so amazing to me that I had spoken a simple word incorrectly for all my life until that point, which made all the difference in the world during conversations with others.

Next on the agenda, my new voice instructor assigned a very short, skinny, nerdy-looking Caucasian male with very thick, square, black-framed glasses as my piano accompanist. The little fellow seemed very timid to me, but when it was time to rehearse the music, he proved to be an awesome pianist. He was always on time for rehearsals and always knew the music planned for that particular day. We highly admired and respected the gifts within each another. One might say that we musically complemented each other.

As time went by, I studied and memorized a total of 21 songs in French, German, Italian, and English for my upcoming music recital. The key word was practice: practice, practice, and practice some more.

SWEET INNOCENT NAIVE

Chapter 13

Sex Before Marriage?

Now it was my junior year in college, and my first and only boyfriend was still in my hometown. I would talk to him via telephone and write him love letters almost every week. I would always be in the dorm when not in class or traveling for the college singing, just waiting for that precious telephone call that I knew was coming from him. Still, there was no intimate relationship with him or anyone else while I was away at college. I can only assume that I really became more curious about the subject of sex because I was always hanging out with the senior girls in college. Even when I was a freshman, since my sister was a senior at the same college, her friends became my friends. Because I was the youngest, they named me "the baby" of the group. No matter where we traveled, I was always referred to as "the baby."

Listening to their many conversations about sex, I became intrigued about the idea, how safe it could be with the proper tools, and what it could do for a relationship. Based on what I had heard the seniors say, I decided that it was time for me to go to that next level in my relationship with my boyfriend. When I traveled home during a holiday break during my junior year of college, I shared my thoughts with my boyfriend. The look on his face was very surprised and shocked, but also delighted to hear this news. He was still a gentleman and he asked me again if this was something that I really wanted to do, because he wanted me to be sure. I assured him that it was indeed my choice because I was in love with him and I would never give this part of me to someone who I did not think that I was in love with; I also told him that I was planning to marry him. It was assumed that we would be married at some point after I got out of college.

This was the Man for Me! The One and Only! This was a man I had known since I was in the 10th grade in junior high school. This was the man who met my parents' requirement of coming to my home to ask my father if he could date me, even though he was really scared of my mother. This was the man whose family my own family knew; they were a good family in our community like my family was too. Therefore, I thought, this had to be the right thing to do. Looking back now, of course, I now know that my mother could read his spirit in ways that I could have never understood at that time.

While I was home for the holiday, we shared a beautiful dinner for two that he had prepared for us at his parents' home while they were out of town. I was a little concerned about going to this next level in our relationship, but I trusted him completely. He was two years older, and in my mind, he was so much smarter about life in general. In my heart, he was my knight in shining armor who would always protect me from anything and anyone. I felt a bond with him that I had never experienced before. I now understand that it's called a "Soul Tie" when you have dived into another level in your relationship with a man.

For about a week afterwards I was still a little fearful about the possibility of getting pregnant, as some girls do after their first time. I could not talk to anyone about this part, though, not anyone at all. I didn't even want my boyfriend to know how afraid I was afterwards because I didn't want to upset him and make him feel guilty about what we had done together. I was so very nervous because in about a week my menstrual cycle was scheduled to start and I knew that to miss my cycle could be very bad news, based on the discussions I had heard between my sister and her senior friends in college.

Each day I would watch the calendar and say a little prayer. My prayer would be, "Lord, please don't let me be pregnant," "please Lord," "please Lord don't make me have to go through that," and then the morning of, my menstrual cycle started as scheduled. WOW! I did not get pregnant! I felt like shouting to the top of my voice, I'm Not Pregnant! I had never been so thrilled for that event to occur within my body before, as much as I hated the pain that it always caused. I called my boyfriend and informed him that I was just fine, though of course I never told him that I was that frightened. The fear for me was all gone! I was delighted and therefore, decided in my heart that it's okay to be intimate, especially with a man you love and planning to marry in the future. He was still a gentleman in this first-time experience for me, so yes in my mind this was the right thing for me to have done.

What was all the fuss about and why was I so fearful? I felt very close to him like never before, but of course I did not know anything about the term "Soul Ties" or the binding of two souls together when you have been intimate with another person. Within my heart I felt as though we were one person, that nothing and no one could come between us, not even my mother who had serious problems with his bad habit of not keeping his word to me. I felt deeply within my heart that he was indeed the man for me, and I knew that I would remain loyal and dedicated to him no matter what. I truly loved him and admired who I had imagined deep within my heart and mind he would become for the future. Based on the way in which he always carried himself, very well-groomed, well-mannered, and articulate, I offered him the highest level of respect, as did others in his presence.

While I was still in college, he joined the military, and I thought to myself, now I've got a Military Man! The uniform just did something to me! What a turn-on! Imagine a tall handsome man with very broad shoulders, the six-pack stomach, muscular arms and legs, and a deep sexy voice, wearing a starched and pressed military uniform. What young naïve girl wouldn't be turned on by that!

SWEET INNOCENT NAIVE

Chapter 14

Cape Hatteras

Pride, Life, Or Death

It was finally the summer before my junior year in college and it was time to prepare for my music recital. This activity was a requirement for all vocal and piano music majors at this particular institution. I was required to memorize songs in French, German, and Italian as well as English for my formal recital that would be reviewed in public, not privately with fellow musicians. A formal recital was similar to preparing for a small one-person concert. The attire requirement was formal evening gowns for the female vocalist or pianist and tuxedos for the male pianist or accompanist.

During the semester with my new voice instructor, I learned to appreciate his very strong personality and the musical challenges that I had conquered with his intense coaching, and I no longer felt intimidated by him. Musically, I truly enjoyed his intense style of coaching; it was an experience that I had not had before as a vocal major, but I thoroughly enjoyed it now. The vocal music intensity for me was similar to playing an intense non-stop game of racket ball. I realized that the level of intensity was what made me "tick" and it was the key that motivated me as a singer. He literally challenged me to be the very best singer I could be. My voice instructor introduced me to some of the most beautiful yet challenging vocal music I had ever been exposed to at that point in my life. He recognized the vocal gift God had blessed me with and he made it his personal goal to "pull" that special gift from God out of me. He described it to me one day as "pushing that baby out of you." I greatly admired and respected him for the push. Personally, I still did not like the smell and the smoking of his pipe, but he was respectful enough to not smoke it as much in my presence. We learned to respect one another with our individual uniqueness.

During the semester, I had met my voice instructor's beautiful wife and their little girl, who was approximately nine or ten years old with red shoulder-length hair and freckles on her face. Together, they were the sweetest little family one could want to meet. His wife was very motherly towards me, he was like a protective father, and their daughter wanted me to be her big sister. Of course, I granted their wishes, much as I had granted my sister and her senior college friends' wish to call me the "baby" of our group.

Just before classes ended for the summer break, my voice instructor informed me that he and his family traveled every summer to a campground they owned located in the Outer Banks of North Carolina. He and his wife invited me to travel with them for the purpose of continuing to prepare the music for my upcoming junior recital. I discussed the matter with my parents and sister, and we made the decision that I would travel that summer with my voice instructor and his family to their campground in the Outer Banks of North Carolina. The only experience I'd had camping was when I was a Brownie in the Girl Scouts at a very young age. I only stayed in the Girl Scouts long enough to get the brownie uniform that we wore with the cute little hat and to stay in the cabins at the state park, where I enjoyed all of the planned activities that summer. That was the extent of my camping experience. But where were the Outer Banks of North Carolina?

Of course I did not know and I really did not care because I was planning to kick up my heels and read a book or two sitting in a lounge chair on the beach wearing my wide straw hat and sunglasses, listen to the music we were preparing for my junior recital on my portable cassette recorder, and celebrate my birthday with my voice instructor and his family. I had the best of both worlds! Fun was first on my agenda and studying my recital music was second. This sounds like the perfect plan to me.

My voice instructor's wife telephoned me and told me to pack summer shorts, shirts jeans, bathing suits, sandals, tennis shoes, and maybe a sweater in case of cool nights, and everything else would be available.

Driving To Cape Hatteras Island

My voice instructor's long old brown station wagon was packed to capacity with all of our summer items and music equipment for the trip. My voice instructor, who in my mind I had taken to calling my new "father" for the summer, took the driver's seat, wearing a wide straw hat, black brim sunglasses with denim grey overalls with a white short-sleeved shirt; dressed like this he looked similar to a farmer, especially with his famous long pipe hanging out of his mouth. His wife, my new "mother" for the summer, took the front passenger seat wearing a cotton dress with a red, white, and blue plaid print, plus white-brimmed sunglasses, a red sun visor, and white sandals. Sitting in the back seat with me was my new little "sister" for the summer, with her head of beautiful red hair and freckles all up her face and arms. She was wearing a pair of orange cotton shorts, with a matching sleeveless orange shirt, white sun visor, and white flip flops, while I was wearing a pair of white silk shorts, a matching white silk short-sleeved shirt, white leather sandals, and a wide straw hat with white square designer sunglasses. Attached to the back of the long brown station wagon was a very long silver Airstream mobile home that the family was going to eat and sleep in once we'd arrived at the campground. My vocal instructor apparently owned a campground for campers only, because hotel accommodations were not available in the area at the time as they are today. I remember thinking to myself, no hotel rooms available? What about my privacy?

As we drove out of the city toward our destination for the summer with the windows down enjoying the sun, not a dark cloud in the bright blue sky and the wind blowing in our faces, I began wondering in my mind, where am I going? I had never in my life heard of Cape Hatteras Island or the Outer Banks of North Carolina. I stared out of the window looking at the beautiful trees and the green grass for mile after miles. The long silver Airstream attached to the back of the station wagon seemed to swing just a little from one side to the other as the car picked up speed. As I mentioned the movement of the mobile home to my summer "mother," she turned around in her seat and assured me that it was normal due to the increase in speed and there was nothing to worry about because my father had it all under control. My voice instructor looked in the rearview mirror at me, nodded his head, and smiled as he continued driving and smoking his long pipe. A little less worried about that now, I began asking questions in reference to how long we would have to travel in order to reach Cape Hatteras, North Carolina. My "father" for the summer looked at me in the mirror for a moment and informed me that the drive would take a few hours, approximately seven to eight, but he assured me that I would really enjoy myself once we arrived. Reassured now, I settled back down in my seat as we traveled through one small town after the other.

During the long drive, we sang songs for a while. Then my mother began reading a book while my little sister and I played several games of Tic Tac Toe, and then we read several funny books together and played with her baby dolls. My little sister looked at the cows out in the field on the side of the highway as I explained to her that when my youngest brother was four or five and he would see cows in the field off of the highway, he would always say to us, "those cows are having a picnic out there."

We drove, and drove, and drove some more, with that long mobile home swinging from one side to the other behind us. We stopped several times at rest stops to stretch our legs, have a picnic lunch that my mother had prepared before leaving home, and pump more gas before hopping back into the car to continue driving, driving, and more driving. My little sister and I took several naps sitting in the back seat with her little head planted in my lap. The wind in my face that once felt so cool and refreshing, was beginning to feel like direct heat from the sun and no one was talking about turning on the air conditioning. I removed my nice straw hat due to the heat and pulled my hair back into a ponytail.

Each time I awakened from my nap, though, we still had not reached our destination. I really wanted to yell, "Are we there yet?" but I decided to stay calm.

Then all of a sudden, we were driving across a very long bridge with a large body of water underneath it; to me, it seemed to stretch as far as the eyes could see. I had never been on a bridge with water underneath that long before and I was absolutely terrified!!!! I was speechless! I remember thinking to myself, I'll be glad when we get to the end of this bridge. It felt like a nightmare even though I was awake, and my eyes were wide open, crossing such a body of water in an old station wagon with a swinging mobile home attached and no help in sight if something happened.

Needless to say, I was indeed terrified!!!! I remember thinking to myself, I cannot swim! I hope this long bridge doesn't break, and I wish that father would decrease the speed of this station wagon with the swinging mobile home attached. I prayed to myself, Lord, please get us to the end of this bridge! I began holding my breath because I was so afraid, but we finally reached the end and I exhaled as he continued driving. I did not mind having to drive more, but I did not want to go across another bridge like that one again.

We kept driving for a while before we finally stopped and approached a boat that was a ferry for people and vehicles that enabled passengers to cross from one side of the island to another. We were directed to approach the ferry boat with our vehicle, and then park and get out of the vehicle. That was a real treat because we were able to stretch our legs again, enjoy the breeze from the wind and I felt safer on the ferry boat crossing the water rather than that long bridge in the car and mobile home.

Cape Hatteras Arrival!

Are we there yet?!?, I continued to scream to myself internally. But finally, after about eight hours driving in that hot old brown station wagon with that long Airstream mobile home swinging from one side to the other behind us and the sun beaming on our faces, we arrived to a place where we could see the beautiful Atlantic Ocean! As we drove through the small village, with only one or two stoplights, there were a couple of small family-owned stores to shop for groceries, several family-owned souvenir shops restaurants and dress shops, one fire department, and many private wooden homes built high up on stilts with screened porches. I had never seen one before other than on television, but a lighthouse was also in view!

Cape Hatteras was a very remote small village. Many of the locals were family members who had never left the area for the city lights and liked it that way. At that time, the area was known for camping and fishing and my voice instructor "father" owned one of the largest campgrounds in the local area.

As we drove into the campground and I looked out the car window, I could see tents of all sizes everywhere; the people around them were mostly Caucasian and of all ages, from young children and teenagers to the middle-aged and elderly. The kids were playing with large striped beach balls, teenagers were playing volleyball, and the men were grilling next to their tents while the women were setting up picnic tables for the family dinners.

The station wagon finally stopped and we all peeled out of the car from the long drive, and my father informed me that I was going to have my very own private pop-up tent! Of course, I did not know what that was, but I was excited that I was going to have some privacy. I had experienced sleeping in a cabin, but I'd never slept in any type of outdoor tent before because I was not an outdoor type of person. After my father detached the long silver Airstream mobile home from the station wagon, we began to empty the car and place items in it. My summer mother and father gathered my pieces of luggage and walked me to the pop-up tent where I would live for the summer, which was near their mobile home. The pop-up tent was so very cute! Off-white in color and just enough room for me! I was simply delighted because it was a wonderful feeling to have my own place to call home. I could stay up all night reading or listening to music if I wanted to without disturbing others. After getting my luggage in the pop-up tent and showing me how everything worked, they gave me a short tour of the campground, which included a game room and gift shop, bathroom areas for men and women with separate shower stalls, and an office where all incoming and outgoing campers would register for a campsite. At the office I was introduced to an older couple, both very short and thin with white hair and glasses, who managed the campground. They were very nice and informed me that they were very happy I was going to spend the summer with them at Cape Hatteras. I felt a very warm welcome from the two of them as well as the other campers as we toured the grounds.

Due to the lateness of the day, my mother prepared dinner in their mobile home and we were done for the day. After dinner I assisted my mother with the dishes before excusing myself and walking to my private pop-up tent nearby. It was wonderful to be able to stretch my legs and relax from the drive. I showered and prepared for bed and climbed on the top bunk bed. As I reflected on the long drive to the Outer Banks, this very peaceful and quite moment was worth the eight hours of hot sun, the swinging of the attached mobile home, and the terrifying long drive across the bridge. While lying in my pop-up tent bed, I could hear the waves as they brushed against each other in the ocean. For me, this moment was similar to lying on the shore and the water slowly flowing over your body so that you don't dare move for interrupting the sheer peacefulness that you are experiencing during that very moment. Every muscle in my body was in a relaxed state; I had never experienced anything like it before, when there was not a moment of tension in my spirit, mind, and body.

    This was the life! WOW! I had never felt such a state of peace. It was as though the sound of the ocean was hypnotizing my spirit, mind, and body. Oh yeah! I told myself. I can do this all summer long, just sitting on the beach!

SWEET INNOCENT NAIVE

Chapter 15

Fair Exchange For Voice Lessons

A few days later, my voice instructor "father" called me into his office and informed me that he had failed to tell me before leaving North Carolina, but I would have to work to pay for my lodging and vocal music lessons. Of course, I said, no problem: what's the job? The word "working" was not a strange term for me because I'd started working at a very early age in life. He informed me that it was an easy job, simply cleaning the shower stalls and bathrooms!

Easy? I thought to myself as I remembered my first day touring those areas. But I had seen that both the men's and women's areas were filthy!!

Needless to say, I was highly insulted, given the fact

that I was a black female in an all-white campground located in a small village environment with no other minorities around. All of a sudden, I was ready to cross that long bridge that had so terrified me just a few days ago and drive eight hours back home because I'd started to experience within my mind and heart what it might have felt like being the only black in an all-white environment; one would call it the "slave mentality" in my mind, cleaning up behind white folks. I began imagining in my mind the same type of pictures that I had seen in the many old classic American movies or Turner films, where black people were always considered to be the "less than" of the human race. People of color weren't considered to be intelligent people but were always portrayed as poor people who were not even allowed to make any decisions for themselves. They were people who did not have any equal rights, and the white man was known as their "Master." The people of color were abused and misused by the white man. Remembering the pictures portrayed in the movies and the history of the black race, I began to feel very insulted, hurt, and disappointed. The person I had begun to respect and admire like a father was now going to treat me, as I saw it, as "less than" others.

There are people in the world who do not mind having a job as a maid and that's ok if that's what you want to do in life, but I was not one of them. I felt belittled and I hated the thought of being made to do this with a passion. An intense level of pride took over in my spirit. I was livid, to say the least. In my heart and mind, based on the old movies that I had seen, I might be labeled as a black maid with a white master or a nanny to their little girl, and I did not want that in any environment.

At the time, I did not share my intense feelings of sheer anger with him; instead I informed him that I would think about it overnight and give him my decision the next morning. I said good night and walked out of his office in the gift shop to my pop-up tent for the night. As I prepared for bed, my heart began to feel very heavy because I felt so very hurt and angry. I could no longer enjoy the beautiful sound of the waves from the ocean, which had given me such a sense of peace and serenity the nights before. While in bed that night, I cried as the tears rolled down my face. I asked myself the question, why didn't he tell me before coming to the Outer Banks, that he wanted me to be a maid and clean up after white folks? In my mind, the answer had to be that he knew that I would not have traveled with them for the summer to prepare for my upcoming music recital. Surely nobody in their right mind would want to clean behind others for any price.

As I thought about the answer to my question, I became more disgusted, disappointed, and hurt by his proposal that he would think of me as a "less than" person. My heart grew heavier the more I thought about the idea of him expecting me to accept such a role. I really believed in my heart that he had higher regard for me than that. He had knocked me off the pedestal I had placed myself on and my ego had blown out of the window into that beautiful ocean. In my opinion, it was ok cleaning my uncle's house as a young girl, but I had matured since that time many years ago and I now thought of myself as a smart young black lady ahead of my hometown high school class. I saw myself as somewhat of a celebrity in my hometown due to my early high school graduation and therefore, permitting me to enter college a year ahead of my classmates, as well as my traveling to Europe having received a music scholarship via the music department at my college. While in Europe, I had shared a room, breakfast, lunch, dinner, tears, joys and defeated challenges with three white girls. We had been like sisters for the summer, and therefore I was certain that I did not have a problem with white people, and I was not prejudiced.

But this man, my "father figure," wanted to treat me like a maid! How dare he! Surely, he had lost his mind! I was convinced that he really did he not understand who I was. I tossed and turned in bed until I was simply outraged by the thought of him asking me to do such a job! I cried even more because this person was really insulting me! I could hardly contain myself, and the tears continued rolling down my face even faster as I wrapped the thought around my brain: the fact that he did not seem to care about who I was and what I had, in my own mind, accomplished thus far in my short life. I got so angry I felt like my body was going to explode! Like the atomic bomb!! There were no family members around for me to talk to about the decision I needed to make, and I did not think to call anyone long-distance to help me make the right decision. The top of my white sheet and white pillowcase both became wet with small smudges of mascara as I continued crying throughout the night.

It seemed like a very long night to me because I thought that my music career was also at stake. I cried so much that I began to experience a headache but suddenly, I knew what to do. I stopped crying and got out of the bed, dried my eyes, blew my nose, and knelt on the floor, where I started praying and asking God what decision I should make. There were many thoughts running through my mind, such as given the fact that my vocal instructor "father figure" was very good at challenging me musically, especially with the level of music I was to perform. Another fact was that he recognized the voice God had blessed me with and he had faith in my becoming a successful opera singer, as well as planning to assist me with the road to opera by getting sponsors to support my career, even though I was still not certain of pursuing a career in opera. Also, thus far he had treated me with the utmost kindness and respect as a person and a young black female.

As I pondered over those thoughts, the Lord spoke to my heart and asked me, What's more important? Your

PRIDE or receiving the very best vocal experience that you have ever received thus far in your life? Also, having someone who knew the ropes of the opera industry, someone who would protect you, and he has only asked you to Earn Your Keep... for the experience. The Lord said to me, "LET YOUR PRIDE GO!" Remember who you are and whom you belong to and do what it takes to have a successful music career. Put on some work clothes, get the job done, then take a shower and change your clothes, and Be Who You Are. You are not a MAID! But a gifted singer. One I have blessed to sing. Cleaning the bathrooms was simply showing me how much you wanted the career in music.

Now, I understand that I needed humility with my God-given gift. I did not understand that I was getting a swelled head!

I thank God for godly parents who taught me how to pray to Him, especially in those times when I felt like there was no one else around that I could go to for guidance.

The next morning, I felt one hundred percent better because I knew that my decision came from God. I got up and prepared a small breakfast of toast, orange juice, two scrambled eggs, and bacon for myself. I got dressed in my red silk shorts and red and black silk shirt, black leather sandals with rhinestones on top, and a black sun visor on my head. I had returned to my peaceful state of mind and I said good morning as I strolled past some of the campers having their morning breakfast. I reached the gift shop and walked up the steps, opening the screen door and entering the main room. As I looked around the room, campers were already playing on the billiard table, ping pong table, and several pinball machines. I noticed in the side room to my left, my voice instructor sitting behind his desk in the office. He was wearing a straw hat, light blue overalls, with a red-and-white striped shirt, reading glasses hanging on the tip of his nose, the village newspaper in his hand. I could smell the fumes from the smoke of that long pipe hanging from his mouth and see a large coffee mug of black coffee sitting on his desk, as I entered his office doorway. We said good morning to each other as he placed his newspaper down to sip the coffee. I informed him that I had given lots of thought to his job proposal and that I had decided to stay for the summer, do the job offered, and learn the music that he had selected for my upcoming music recital. He said that's great! So, let's get started!

To this day, I never shared with him nor anyone else how his initial job offer made me feel because I had heard from God on the matter. The drama was over.

The summer was going great! My schedule included cleaning the shower stalls and bathrooms, and then private lessons studying fantastic music with my voice instructor. Every evening just before the sun would go down, I had a lounge chair out on the beach, where I would sit and read or listen to music until dark.

Chapter 16

Surprise Birthday Dinner

This particular day we were going to celebrate my birthday. Everyone seemed to have known it was my birthday because all during the day, different campers would say "Happy Birthday" to me; the manager and his wife even gave me a beautiful seashell from the local gift shop. My vocal instructor's wife, "my mother figure" for the summer, had been bubbly all day long and said that she could not wait until dinner because she had something special prepared just for me. When I had completed my tasks for the day, I changed clothes for dinner. I entered the Airstream mobile home for dinner and to my surprise, my "mother" had prepared a pot of black-eyed peas and a pan of cornbread for my surprise birthday dinner! To her surprise, though, I did not eat black-eyed peas and cornbread. As a matter of fact, I absolutely hated black-eyed peas and cornbread even though I was black. As kids, we were made to eat what was on our dinner plate on the table, but this was one dish that I had never enjoyed eating. I had declared that once I was old enough, I would never eat black-eyed peas again. So now I explained to her how appreciative I was of the thought but not all black people eat black-eyed peas and cornbread. As preachers' kids, we had always been taught to show appreciation for what was presented to us, but also to be gracious when declining something as an act of kindness. Of course, she was disappointed because she had prepared such a special meal just for my birthday. However, I was able to eat the white rice and green beans that she had prepared with the black-eyed peas and cornbread.

Along with the dinner, I received a beautiful silver and gold bracelet that wrapped around my wrist; the wristband was made of metal that looked like long fingers wrapping around one's wrist. I still have the bracelet in my jewelry box from that birthday so many years ago. It truly was a very special day for me.

During the summer months at the Cape Hatteras campground, I enjoyed studying and preparing the music for my upcoming vocal music recital and fishing at the beach with my vocal instructor and summer "father" as well as his daughter, my "red-haired and freckle-faced little sister," while my instructor's wife and summer "mother" remained at the mobile home preparing our dinner for the evening. As a young girl, I had only seen my grandmother fish from a pier, and she was considered an expert based on the number of catches she had made at the end of each trip. But my personal fishing skills were limited to throwing the fishing rod in the ocean and catching the fish with the rod while my voice instructor would put the bait on the rod and take the fish off the fishing rod for me after each catch. I was afraid of touching the slimy wiggly bait and the mouth of the fish once I had caught it. The only part of the adventures of fishing that I enjoyed was casting the rod into the ocean, feeling the line on the rod pull when there was a fish at the end of the line, and the process of reeling the fish to shore. This process was very exciting to me because the capture of the fish was a challenge accomplished. But the closer the fish got to me during the reeling in, the more I was ready to drop the fishing rod and run. Even though my little sister was very young, she was already good at catching fish due to her early experience.

There were days when I had completed my chores and studying my music for the day, that my sister and I would put on our tennis shoes and run several miles up to the light house and have fun walking down the beach until dinner time. Cape Hatteras was a very private area during those days, not at all commercialized as it is today with its many tourists and hotels. We would walk along the beach without seeing a lot of people, only occasionally a fisherman or two. The atmosphere was very calm, relaxed, and easy-going.

At that time, Cape Hatteras would have been the perfect place for retirees and businessmen/women who wanted to get away from the hustle and bustle of life. In the small village, the treat for every other weekend was the local fire department's fish dinners, which were held to raise money for different fundraising projects. The fish dinners included large pieces of fish that covered my dinner plate, a choice of beautiful golden-brown hush puppies or dinner rolls, homemade potato salad, and tossed green salad with home-grown tomatoes, and thick, chewy homemade chocolate brownies with sweet iced tea. After such a delicious meal, there was nothing left to do for the day but sit in a lounge chair on the beach, listening to the waves brushing up against each other as I slowly drifted off into a deep sleep. This was truly a peaceful way of living.

Chapter 17

Eye Of The Hurricane

While at Cape Hatteras, the summer days continued being the perfect temperature, not too hot and not too cold, and each brought that ultimate sense of serene peacefulness. That is, until one day we received a frightening weather report via the news on the radio. The radio announcer's weather report stated that the eye of a hurricane was scheduled to hit Cape Hatteras, North Carolina at 8:30 a.m. that coming weekend.

Suddenly, the atmosphere among the people changed from a serene happy-go-lucky feeling to one of sheer panic. Everyone on the Island was informed by the authorities that we should evacuate before the storm's arrival. Campers were gathering up their camping equipment, loading the vehicles with their families, and filling their cars with gas in order to drive as far away as possible to safety. As the campers drove away with mobile homes and pop-up tents attached, they waved good-bye to us.

I had no doubt in my mind that shortly we would be packing and leaving as well. My "father" was the owner of the campground, so of course it was his responsibility to make sure all of the campers were getting out safely and then everything would be nailed down to keep the wind and rain from destroying the property. My new friends, the couple that managed the campground, were also packing their vehicle preparing to leave with the rest of the Island evacuees. They gathered as much as possible because, based on the weather report, they did not know how long they would be gone and how much destruction would occur.

When the weekend arrived, the sun in the sky slowly began to disappear within the clouds, as the day grew darker and the wind blew stronger. The white plastic chairs began to roll from picnic tables that had not been tied down as the rain began falling. Several other campers were in the gift shop with us listening to the weather report on the radio when suddenly a young couple opened the gift shop door and ran through in a state of panic. The young man's head had been injured while trying to dismantle their little tent for two in the process of preparing to evacuate the island. His young wife was crying due to pain in her leg from attempting to assist her husband in dismantling their tent. I remembered meeting this couple upon their registration for a campground site, because everyone was so excited that they were newlyweds at Cape Hatteras for their honeymoon. The young wife was very upset because of what she and her new husband had experienced simply attempting to get to safety in the campground office. Luckily, my "mother" was able to get the emergency first aid kit and attend to their injuries.

While she did, I looked out of the window and saw that it was beginning to rain harder as the wind increased even more. I asked my "father," wasn't it time for us to pack our things and prepare to evacuate as well, but he informed me that we were not going to be leaving!!!!!

I looked into his eyes, then I looked to the left at my mother and my little sister who never said a word on the matter, and then I turned back to him and I asked, what do you mean we are not going to be leaving? He quietly informed me once again "We were not going to be leaving the campground!"

When I asked him why not, he informed that he could not leave his property that had taken him years to build as a retirement business for he and his family's future. Therefore, leaving was not an option. I took a deep breath as tears began to well up in my eyes. The property manager and his wife were standing on my right side, and I looked at them and begged them to take me with them to safety.

They informed me that they would love to take me, but they did not have permission from my "father", and he was not going to allow them to take me because I was his responsibility, not theirs.

I pleaded and begged the property manager and his wife again to take me with them because my voice instructor insisted on staying and riding the storm out because he owned this campground and they were not going to leave the property. The property was his "little baby" that was so special to him that my life and safety did not matter! The property manager and his wife explained to me once again that they were very sorry but because I arrived with my voice instructor and his family, they were responsible for me and therefore, they were not able to take me with them.

As I watched them drive out of the campground without me, I WAS A WRECK!!! I stood on the porch still in a state of shock! This was my last chance gone down the tubes, to physically leave a location that was targeted for the eye of a hurricane! I could not believe I was being left behind to endure this life or death situation, simply because someone had not given permission to allow me to leave and get to safety. That way of thinking did not make any sense to me at all!

To walk around in the gift shop during the storm, we used flashlights and candles because the electricity had gone out and therefore, the telephone lines were down. With the telephone lines being out of order, I could not make any calls to my family to let them know that my life was in danger and that I needed someone to come and rescue me. I feared that I did not have any hope of living once I knew I did not have a way to escape the danger that was reportedly on its way. Now that I think about it, I was not mature enough at the time to insist on finding a way to leave. I had never experienced either a hurricane or a tornado before, so needless to say, I felt helpless and hopeless and I was not a happy camper. Not. At. All.

The campground was evacuated but several campers decided to stay on the Island with us. There was a total of nine of us who remained on the campground to weather the eye of storm. My voice instructor "father" and his male friends drove through the campground in the increasing rain and wind to complete a final check and make sure everything was as secure as possible. It was then decided by my father that the safest place for all of us to spend the night would be in the gift shop. So, everyone got their assigned sleeping areas in the gift shop, not knowing whether or not we would awaken the next morning. My assigned sleeping area for the night was on the top of the billiard table. I placed my blankets and pillows on the table, which was still very hard but at least I was not on the floor. Due to the possibility of water overflowing in the building, I felt a little safer up on the billiard table than I would be sleeping on the floor. We were all fully dressed due to the lack of privacy and given flashlights and candles in order to see during the night, like if we were trying to get to the restroom. Dressed in my blue jeans, sweatshirt, and tennis shoes, I climbed on top of the billiard table, laid my head on the two pillows, and covered my body with a blanket. I was still in a state of shock that I was left behind and had no way to get to safer grounds. Everyone said goodnight to each other as we settled in for the night, fearing for our lives. Then everyone was secure in their assigned sleeping areas, and all the candles and flashlights were cut off for the night.

It was a very long, dark, and stressful time for me because all during the night I could hear nothing but the sound of the wind, the heavy downpour of the rain, and the increasingly loud sounds of the raging water from the ocean. I could not believe that we could not make any telephone calls out to our family members at a time when we were all very desperate, with the exception of my voice instructor. I still could not believe that he thought more about his precious campground than our lives. During the night, I tossed and turned on the hard-billiard table, jumping up several times when things hit the side of the building. I broke out into cold sweats during the night because I heard whistling sounds from the outside that I had never heard before. I concluded that the only thing left for me to do was to pray to God for a while, hoping and trusting in Him that we would be alive the next morning, all while still remembering in the back of my mind that the weather report stated that the eye of the hurricane was surely going to hit where we were staying. What I understood from this at the time was that we were physically located in the very eye of the storm and that it was going to take a miracle from God for us to survive.

As the night grew longer, I finally cried myself off to sleep with the thought that I was unable to make contact with my family to say goodbye and that we might not awaken the next morning. It was very difficult to sleep due to debris from the heavy rain and winds consistently hitting on the sides of the building. There were moments during the night that I laid there hugging a pillow with a heavy heart in a very quiet and hopeless state of mind, staring up at the ceiling as tears continued rolling down my face.

I must have cried myself to sleep, though, because to my surprise, I opened my eyes and I saw beautiful sunlight flowing through the room! I raised my head from my pillow and looked around the room and I realized – it was the next morning and we were still alive! God had answered my prayer! Everyone else began to arise from their assigned sleeping areas in the room as we rejoiced hugging each other because we had lived through the night and it was the next morning after 8:30 A.M!

As a group we walked out of the gift shop to survey the damage outside. As we picked our way through the campground, we saw that there was lots of debris, like tables and chairs scattered because they had not stay tied down. We reached the Airstream and everything seemed to be intact. When we reached my pop-up tent, we found that the storm had turned the tent upside down. Even though the sun was very beautiful and bright, the campground felt like a ghost town because there were only nine of us left there. To me, the atmosphere was similar to the Valley of Death, even though no one had died, you knew in your spirit that destruction had taken place there.

Later, the authorities of the village came by and informed us that the eye of the hurricane had gone 40 miles out to sea instead of hitting our direct location as the weather reports had predicted. Of course, we were all delighted to be alive, but I was very disappointed that my voice instructor "father" would not allow me to leave with his managers who had left for safety. I could not believe that he would jeopardize my life when he only needed to give his permission for me to leave.

In my own way, though, I simply got over it. I think I simply decided that he knew what was best for me and that I was his responsibility, not his managers'. The incident did not make me feel good about his decision, but I simply accepted what happened. I was not mature enough to fight for the safety of my very own life.

Eventually, though, the summer finally ended. All songs in English, German, French, and Italian had been memorized, and now we just had to get back to campus and put the final touches on each song with the private pianist who had been assigned to me.

This was a trip that I will never forget. I had passed the Pride Test and the Fear Test! But also, I had slept, eaten, and breathed music for several months, and I was now convinced that opera was the career path for me. Music was now within my spirit so much that due to excitement I had forgotten about the extra weight that in Austria I had been told was a requirement. In fact, the subject never came up with my private voice instructor.

Putting a career of music first versus getting married and having a family also never came up in our conversations. For my future, there would be lots of challenging music to be learned, and lots of people within the music industry to be introduced to via my voice instructor. I had decided within my mind, that he was not only my voice instructor but would also serve as the manager of my career in the music industry. I truly believed in my heart that he would protect me from all the hurt, harm, and dangers that had scared me before, based on what I had observed and felt during my experience while studying in Europe. In my mind, I had the very best vocal instructor in the world, and everything would be fine!

SWEET INNOCENT NAIVE

Chapter 18

Attack Of The Devil

During the winter of my senior year in college, I attended a music major's conference on my college campus. When the conference had ended for the day, I reached into the coat closet, pulled out my coat, and left. By that evening, my left hand had swollen and was a bright red color. My hand was so swollen and itched so badly that I was continuously scratching it, unable to even put a glove on it.

At first it appeared as though I had been bitten by maybe a spider that may have been in the coat closet. But the swelling continued every other week. My feet, lips, and eyes were shut tight, my face would be unrecognizable, and every part of my body would seem to swell at different times, from my ears to my abdomen, head, legs, and chest.

Needless to say, I was absolutely miserable. I took medication for different allergies; rub-down alcohol, cold and hot pads, a tub of cold water, and anything else that might stop the itching. My personal doctor put me on a diet to see if there was something I may have been eating that was causing the swelling. I kept a list of foods eaten, the time and date eaten, and the results, but we learned nothing from this. Worse, my doctor informed me that if I ever had a problem with my tongue swelling, I should get to the hospital emergency room as soon as possible because it could kill me. The news of that caused me even more stress, because then I began to be afraid of falling asleep, not knowing if I would wake up the next day because I had been unable to breathe during the night due to my tongue swelling. And nothing in my list of foods seemed to be unique that would have caused an allergic reaction.

Finally, my doctor placed me in the hospital at Bowman Gray in North Carolina to run tests of every kind. I'd never been in the hospital before for myself – u I was always the one going to assist or visit others in the hospital and therefore this was going to be a major experience. I hated needles and when I was younger, I had run from the doctor when as kids we had to get vaccination shots; they had to come and find me. So, needles were not friends of mine. Now, seven test tubes of blood were being taken from my body, though this only succeeded when they finally got someone in the room who could get the blood from my left arm, not my right, because my veins were so small. Once this task was accomplished, test tubes of blood went to Chapel Hill and to Duke University for testing.

I stayed in the hospital for a week with 17 doctors parading back and forth out of my room asking the same questions trying to find out why I was swelling, or what was causing me to swell up. Finally, I asked one doctor to repeat what I'd said to him to the next doctor coming into my room because I was tired of repeating the story. But that did not work; I had to start the story all over again. I realized much later that they were trying to see if there was anything different in my story that may have given them some clues to what was causing the swelling in any part of my body at any time. Did it occur while I was happy, sad, or a non-emotional state of mind?

When the blood test results returned, they indicated absolutely nothing strange in my blood. After a week's stay in the hospital and them running all kinds of tests, the only result I received was a cold and a sore throat because the room was too cold.

As several years passed, I continued to swell up in different parts of my body. My body would swell up so often that it became difficult for me to make plans for going out with friends or to leaving town for the weekend. I became paranoid about what I would eat. I would swell up if I was happy and I would swell up if I became sad, so

I was on a mental roller coaster ride trying not to have any kind of emotions for fear of triggering the swelling in my body. I became very withdrawn and detached. There were times when I could not go to church because my face or eyes were swollen, which was unbearable for me. My skin where the swelling occurred would be so swollen tight that it was very painful, and I could not even bend my fingers or wiggle my toes. I did lots of crying myself to sleep. This pain was so dreadful and so much that I would not have wished it on my worst enemy. I had to reach even deeper in praying, fasting, and begging God to heal me.

This attack on my body came out of nowhere and lasted for several years. I had never had any medical history of being sick with anything in my life, and I had never been in the hospital other than for testing for this swelling problem. My family and I went from putting me in a chair at the church and allowing the elders and missionaries of the church pray for me sitting in the circle to my mother taking me to see her aunt who lived in Georgia. Her aunt had a special gift for helping people who were told someone had witchcraft placed upon them. My mother's aunt, who had a special gift for helping people, informed my mother that someone had indeed performed witchcraft upon me without my knowledge. She described the person as well as the situation and then she gave me a special cloth to pin on my shirt and wear next to my body. She also had me drink a liquid product that had a very bitter taste, which she had created to defeat the witchcraft that she was certain someone had placed upon me.

This was a calling in her life that she had performed for many years, but I'd never been aware of it until my mother got desperate enough to discuss who she was with me. I'd remembered as a young child visiting her and one day as I was coming down the stairs in her two-story brick home, her maid put her arm out and tried to trip me. To this day, I do not know why. No one believed me at that time because she was an adult, I was a child, and no one saw the incident. I also remember lots of people coming in and out of my mother's aunt home when we were visiting, but at the time I was not old enough to inquire as to what was going on. I now know why they were there: they were all waiting to receive her help. My mother did not really believe in her aunt's power/gift, but we were all so absolutely desperate to resolve this problem, which was not just my problem but a family problem that none of us had ever heard of before.

I was climbing the walls because absolutely no one could help me with this sickness. I kept saying to myself, why was I having this sickness? What did I do to deserve this problem? I was always nice to everybody. I was never ever sick growing up other than the normal children's diseases like chicken pox, measles, and the mumps. I thrived on having a perfect attendance in elementary school. Even when I was playing in my uncle's truck and cut my knee so that I had to have 19 stitches in my kneecap, I got on my crutches and insisted that my mother take me to school. That's how healthy I was, so I just did not understand at all why this was happening to me. There were times I just did not want to live like this anymore because it was unfair to me and to my family for all of us to have to endure such a fate.

One weekend while at my parent's home, my face had swollen up and I was lying in bed with a cold hand towel partially covering my face. My dad stopped by my room just to check on me, and he could not tell that I was watching him because my eyes were so swollen that one could not tell that my eyes were even open. My dad just stood at the door looking helpless because he simply did not know how to resolve this problem: his baby girl was in pain and he could not do anything to help ease it for her. I was later informed that my father's brother was at our house while my face was swollen and he felt that he was not strong enough to see me looking the way I was looking, "like a monster." I got to the point that I was afraid to even say the word "swelling" for fear that it would happen again once it had gone down. The swelling of all parts of my body continued during my senior year in college, through my year of graduate school, and during and after my first professional job.

Chapter 19

Encounter With Good & Evil

One particular night when I was staying at my parent's home, my right hand up to my elbow was swollen. I had been praying and had fallen asleep with my small bible on top of my stomach. During that night all of a sudden, my room got very hot – even though it had been a very cool night – but suddenly, I realized my hand was on my stomach. In one of my ears I heard a voice say, "A-ha, I got you," and then I heard a voice say, "You choose, the devil or Jesus." At that moment I saw something come from my stomach like the picture of atomic bomb commercials that I'd seen on TV.

I struggled to speak, but it was as though something was holding my mouth tightly together and my teeth felt like they were in a locked position. I kept struggling to move my lips in order to make a sound and I was finally able to say the word "Jesus!" After I was able to speak the word *Jesus*, to this day I have no memory of getting out of the bed, leaving my bedroom, and walking down the hallway from my bedroom to my parents' bedroom to get into their bed. But somehow, I woke up the next morning sleeping in between my parents. I told them what had happened in my room during the night and my parents did not seem to remember my getting in the bed with them either.

It has now been many years since that happened, but I still do not remember leaving one bedroom and going to another bedroom that was down the hall and around the corner from where I was sleeping, as frightened as I was on that night. I remember being very afraid, not only to move but afraid to even breathe! For a short time after that experience, I was afraid of walking in a dark room. I would reach for the light switch on the wall to turn the lights on before going into a room.

But eventually I asked God to take that fear of the darkness away from me and He did. I knew that the devil wanted to keep me fearful.

Chapter 20

Christmas Morning

One Christmas morning, I had awoken earlier than the rest of the family, but when I went to the restroom and looked in the mirror, my face was so swollen that no one would have recognized me; I was absolutely devastated and miserable.

Christmas mornings were always, always special in our parents' home. My parents and my older sister would always be up before the rest of us. They would go from room to room singing "Jingle Bells" very loudly with tambourines to wake up any family member in the bedroom, and if your head was under the covers, they would continue singing and pull one of your legs out from under the covers until they were successful at getting you out of the bed and joining them in their Christmas morning sing-a-long to go and awaken the next victim in the next bedroom. This was our Christmas morning family tradition. Then when everyone was out of bed, we'd all go downstairs in our pajamas to the family room, daddy would say the family prayer, and my younger brothers and I would be in charge of passing out the gifts. Each gift had a family member's name on it and some gifts were gag gifts so of course we were always excited to see who got the gag gifts this Christmas morning. One never knew what was in the package, based on the box. Gag gifts were the most fun when you saw the priceless look on the recipient's face.

But this particular Christmas, when I realized my face was so badly swollen, I got back into bed, totally depressed and crying because I knew that it would put a damper on our family's Christmas morning tradition, which was always lots of fun! I hated being the one to destroy our morning of fun. I told God that I no longer wanted to live if I had to live with this swelling problem. Any part of my body would swell up at any time; there was no pattern and no cause for it that the doctors could really determine.

On this particular Christmas morning, I went into the bathroom again before anyone could come to my room and looked into the mirror one more time. But this time, when I looked directly into my own eyes that were so swollen that I could only peep, I saw the enemy. I saw something in my eyes that I really could not put into words other than that it was the enemy.

After much torment from the swelling in the different areas of my body, prayer at church with the prayer warriors, and fasting, I finally stopped using the items that my mother's aunt had developed for me because our family did not believe in witchcraft. It was then that I realized that this had come from the devil attacking my body. So, I decided to trust God.

I started consuming the word of God with healing scriptures. I also began fighting the devil by verbally telling him that I belonged to God, that he has no authority over my body because my body belongs to God and not him, and declaring that I was healed and not sick on a daily bases. Then, the swelling all of a sudden stopped! I don't even remember the exact date that it stopped, I just know that the fight was on and I won. I put on the whole armor of God. I understood the fact that not only can your family pray for you, but you, the person being attacked, must stand up and fight the devil yourself. The devil's job is to kill, steal, and destroy, and he will if you allow him to. GOD IS THE HEALER BUT WE HAVE TO BELIEVE THAT HE IS THE HEALER. We have to know that all healing took place on the cross, so it's already done! For the believers!

If you have not given your life to Christ, it's never too late, simply repeat these words: Dear Lord Jesus, I believe in You in my heart. I know that I have sinned, and I need You. I sincerely from my heart ask for Your forgiveness and love. I ask You to cleanse my heart, mind, and life from all unrighteousness. Direct my footsteps from this day forward. Today, I receive You within my heart as my Lord and Savior, so I can enjoy the abundant life that You won for me on the Cross. Amen.

Welcome to the Family of God!

Chapter 21

Undergradute College Graduation

    Now it was finally the end of my senior year! Time for graduation! No more choir rehearsals, no more memorizing 20+ songs in four languages for music recitals, no more music theory and music history classes, no more college choir, no more singing at programs traveling with the college quartet staying in the Playboy hotel for Free in Chicago, no more eating what we all called on our college campus "wonder meat" in the cafeteria! No more, no more!

    And guess what! This would also be the very first time that my boyfriend had come to visit! I was always going home for the holiday or talking to him via telephone or writing letters, but now he was actually coming to campus and I was so excited that I could have burst!

To this day, I am still not sure what happened, but I have been left with a very strong impression that someone in my family twisted his arm in order for him to show up. Part of why I suspect this is because he had never come for a visit before. He had made promises many times, but it had never happened and I think that someone in my family decided that they were not going to allow him to disappoint me this time. No one has never really told me, but when I think about it, plus some of the whispers that I have heard when no one knew that I was around, I really think that this is what happened.

At any rate, graduation was great!!!!! Everybody who I wanted to be there was there!

Imagine That!

It was a "No Drama" Weekend for me!

Chapter 22

Home For The Summer

Now it was time to go home after college. I decided to get a job for the summer until I could decide whether or not I should go on to graduate school. As I was trying to make this decision, I spoke to family members and friends about what I should do. Everyone thought that I should continue my education, except my boyfriend. He informed me that I had left him behind before while I was away in college for four years, and he did not think that I should leave him again. While at home during the summer after graduation, it had taken the better part of the summer before I was really able to secure a summer job. Therefore, I was really torn as to whether or not I should go to pursue a master's degree or else just keep the job that I had finally gotten. But after lots of thinking and discussing my concerns with people such as my parents, my sister who was already working in a successful career, and former high schoolteachers who were next-door neighbors to my parents, I made a final decision to continue my education and go to graduate school.

I informed my boyfriend of my decision; after all, this was still the young man I'd started dating when I was in the 10th grade. He said ok, if that's what you really want to do, but he'd rather I stay in our small hometown. In the meantime, he had only accomplished going to the military and he had no job after getting out – nothing that was of any substance according to my standards and the standards of those individuals whose opinions I respected highly. Finally, though, he agreed that I should go on and pursue graduate school even though he really did not want me to go. But he had nothing better to offer.

Young women should always listen to their mother or someone with wisdom when it comes to their first boyfriend. I had always admired and respected this man, but he'd always have dreams and was never pursuing them. It had become a pattern with him that my mother had tried to point out to me several times. He talked a lot without words of substance. But I still loved him, and thought he was my one and only love!

How foolish of me.

Chapter 23

Destiny Killer

I completed the summer job in my hometown as a salesclerk in a major department store, then packed my bags again, said my goodbyes to everyone including my boyfriend, and went off to graduate school.

Disappointed because I was unable to continue vocal private lessons with my undergraduate vocal music instructor, I was assigned to a vocal music graduate school instructor at a new university. This changed everything for me because this new vocal music instructor could not relate to my personality. She was unable to relate to my God-given unique vocal gift that had been acknowledged by others during my undergraduate years. I had been so well trained and nurtured during my undergraduate experiences that many believed I should have pursued a career in opera. But this new instructor did not select challenging music for me to perform, and worst of all, she assigned me music that was written for a mezzo soprano instead of a lyric soprano.

This was devastating for me. As a music student who had always received the academic grade of "A," now I was receiving the academic grade of "D" in the subject of voice. I wonder why? The experience with this new voice instructor was so disgusting for me that I would call in sick so that I would not have to endure the experience of studying under her direction. The whole bad experience changed the direction of my career, leading me to simply complete one year of graduate school and completely give up on the idea of pursuing a career in opera. Due to my level of immaturity it did not enter my mind that I should fight for what I really wanted at the time, such as fighting for a new voice instructor or fighting to return to working with my former vocal instructor, the person who understood who I was. I should have fought for the person who was putting me on a career track that could have been successful and the person who believed in me and what God had placed within me.

This new graduate school voice instructor never knew how she negatively impacted my life. She had a very non-caring personality and did not care that she did not challenge me with the music she had selected for me to study. I enjoyed more complex styles of music that were very intense. Worse, she had also selected the wrong voice part for me; I am a lyric soprano, not a mezzo soprano. This instructor was simply the wrong fit for me, which devastated me so much that I simply gave up on my destiny.

The moral of this experience is to Fight Back for Your Destiny! Never let someone else's lack of knowledge and abilities determine your destiny. Understand who you are and what your abilities are and make an effort to get sound advice from someone with wisdom. And always, always FIGHT BACK! Don't give up!

This was not the only problem I encountered during that year, though. As a graduate student worker in the music department, I was given the opportunity to work part-time between classes in the music department library. My job was to file sheet music and books in their proper places as well as create labels for filing the newly arrived books. During this job, several of us worked in the library with a supervisor who was a student just a little older than we were. This student supervisor was very short and somewhat on the plump side; she had a large mole on the right side of her face, and a couple of her teeth were missing. She wore black square-brimmed glasses, and her auburn hair was always held together with a wide red rubber band on her long ponytail. Most of the time she would wear a pair of jeans and a sweatshirt with dirty white tennis shoes. Everyone attempted to treat her with kindness even though she had a very curt and ice-cold personality. Ignoring her personality, we were all getting along just fine, completing our work and discussing our classes. After some time, though, all of a sudden, the student supervisor began accusing several of us of misfiling books and sheet music; at the same time, items were being misplaced within the library. Everyone was confused that this was suddenly happening, and that the student supervisor was always the person to locate all missing items. Several of us quit the job because we were being falsely accused and unable to prove our innocence.

One of our friends who had not been accused and continued working in the music department library later informed us that the manager of the music library discovered that the student supervisor had a jealous and envious personality. She was also found guilty of hiding materials on the top of shelves in order to make it look as though others were misfiling and misplacing materials; she was caught in the act and of course immediately fired.

Again, the moral of this story is also to Fight Back when you know that someone is lying and trying to discredit your name. Take the time to prove them wrong by getting to the bottom of the situation instead of just throwing your hands up in the air and walking away. Do not give up or give in just because the person has seniority or is the supervisor. In this case, that did not change the fact that she was a liar. It was only by the grace of God that she got caught in the act and we were proven innocent. Truth will prevail!

SWEET INNOCENT NAIVE

Chapter 24

Love And Graudate School

During my time in graduate school, I would maintain contact with my boyfriend in my hometown. We consistently made contact either via telephone, letters, or cards. Then all of a sudden, he stopped calling and I was unable to reach him at home via telephone. When it was time for me to go home for a holiday break and I returned to our house, my mother called me into her room, where she informed me that she had learned from a reliable source that my boyfriend was now married and had been married for 3 months, due to feeling he needed to do what was considered to be honorable with a young lady – get married. His parents were Christian and thought that was the right thing to do.

When my mother told me this news, I simply felt numb; I don't think I was able to allow the news to sink in at that moment. This man was someone I had started dating when I was in the 10th grade up to my first year of graduate school. He was the first and only man that I had been physically and emotionally involved with because I was in love with him and was planning to marry him. This was the man who I had planned to one day be the mother of his children, and we were going to grow old together. Even though I was many miles away from him while in undergraduate and graduate school, I had remained faithful to our relationship and trusted him, AND NOW HE WAS MARRIED TO SOMEONE ELSE! Oh No!!!! This could not be true.

My mother explained to me that this information had come from someone who was related to him, who then informed someone related to my mother. Both of these people were very reliable, and therefore, could be believed.

This became the worst moment of my life. I asked myself, how could this happen to me after so many years? What could have changed? I had all kinds of questions in my mind. I fasted and prayed for 8 months from morning to noon without telling my family. I was not living in my hometown during this time but I was close enough to drive to my parents' home for the weekend. This made the fasting during the week easier for me to continue and keep from my family because I would eat during the weekend while at my parents' home.

During the whole experience, I went into a type of shell, just like a crab would go into his hard shell to protect himself, so even though I was functioning daily, I felt like a zombie. I felt like I was going to lose my mind! There were times when I would leave to return to where I was living during the week due to work, which was approximately 80 miles away. While I was on the highway driving at high speed in my sports car, the devil whispered in my ear to just let go of the steering wheel. This happened several times while traveling.

I did not know my strength at that time, but I did not listen to the voice of the devil. My heart felt like someone had taken a knife and was twisting it in there. I did not understand it at that time, but I was grieving due to the death of a relationship that I'd truly believed was meant to be even though I did not have any other relationship to measure it by. I simply felt like dying because I was so devastated by what had occurred. Many times, I grabbed the Bible and started to read and cry. There were times that my eyes were so full of tears that I could not see the words I was attempting to read. After many moments of crying and reading the Bible, I finally got a grip and decided that it was time to talk with this man because I was certain that he did not love the woman he was now married to. I believed within my heart that he had married her because he was expected to do the honorable thing. I admired him for wanting to take care of his responsibility.

It was very painful for me to learn of all the activities that were occurring, which looked like a family was being formed with ease and no consideration for me and my feelings, even when I was in the area to see it taking place. I felt as though it as all an attempt to torment me, so I simply focused on praising God and not the situation trying to distract me in church of all places. I completed my first year of graduate school, got a job, and moved near my hometown in order to be close to the person I still viewed as my boyfriend who was now married to someone he was not in love with. In my naivety, I believed, based on what I had been told, that the new relationship with this other woman would be dissolved. I never told my parents that I had such expectations because they would not have agreed. Furthermore, my parents were not aware of the fact that I was feeling this intense devastation because I was able to hide my true feelings. I was very close to some of the family who were as confused by this situation as I was. More time went by and the marriage was still intact. I remained hopeful of a renewed relationship based on discussions we had shared for a future, even in the midst of the now 8-month-old marriage.

It was not until I received a special telephone call from a reliable source that I finally realized there was a double-sided plan at work – one real plan in the making and another fantasy plan conveyed to me with absolutely no plan of action to be realized. The person on the phone was informing me that the man I still believed was my soul mate (my first and only love, the man I was planning to marry and have a family with) was at that very moment at my grandfather's home, since he was also their pastor. The couple was presently in my grandfather's office discussing their plans of how to work things out "together"! Or "How they wanted to keep their little family together!"

In my immature/naive mind, when did they become a family? What happened with the two of them and this little child he now had, becoming a family? This was the last straw for me! I was absolutely devastated. It was my moment of recognizing it was never going to happen! What happened to the promises made to me?

Ok, I said to myself, it's time to let go of him now.

Getting over this hurt took lots of crying, fasting, praying, reading the Bible, reading books that consist of daily encouragement or comfort, and asking God to heal my spirit, mind, and body. I literally begged God to take my intense love for this person out of my heart. This took several years of begging God to help me let go of him in my heart, not just in my head. Several years passed and I still had a wonderful relationship with his mother and other members of that family. I was not mature enough to know it at that time, but a dream of the future with this person still somewhere in my heart. Several more years passed, during which I matured and finally understood that I had to also let go of his family members, whom I had been very close to over the years. I gradually realized that I had been holding on to his family as a way of holding onto a person who was now married and was planning to stay married. I think what kept me holding on to this dream was the fact that I believed he did not love her and I thought that because he loved me; his marriage to her would not last. In my mind, his love for me was stronger than anything else.

After much fasting, praying, reading the Bible and other books on subjects of comfort, encouragement, and my own maturing, I finally realized that if my ex-boyfriend had really loved me, he would not have been with the young lady in the first place while I was away at college. He would have been as faithful to me as I was to him and he would have discussed the situation with me when the mistake occurred, instead of allowing me to walk into such devastation. He would not have never ever thought about marrying her or allowed anyone to pressure him into marrying someone just because of external cultural pressures. He would have married me if he really loved me, no matter what the circumstance were. I had to accept the truth in my head and my heart, which was "He really did not love me." He liked me, but based on his actions, real love was not in his heart.

A word to young ladies, love is an action word. Don't allow the young man to simply say he loves you but never show it in his actions towards you. Pray to God, look for a man's actions, and get married first. My healing took shape as I matured and found forgiveness in my heart for all parties who had contributed to my pain, including myself.

SWEET INNOCENT NAIVE

Chapter 25

Letting Go

I finally accepted the truth within my heart and I was able to completely let go of him. That experience forced me to get closer to God through intense times of fasting, praying, reading books of comfort/encouragement, and reading the Bible.

Letting go was what I had to learn as my life's journey evolved, beginning as a teenager through the early years of adulthood. The effects of betrayal and the loss of truth can negatively impact your life if you allow this to happen.

Maturity, or lack of it, is an experience that can shape your entire future if you do not accept the truth when circumstances in your life knock on your door. The greatest lesson I learned in such moments, when circumstances in my life occurred that impacted decisions I made for myself, was deciding to let go.

Several years later, I was informed by a reliable source that the precious little baby boy was not actually my ex-boyfriend's child, so he and the lady he had married instead of me were finally separated. About 10 years later, my ex-boyfriend called me at my workplace located many hours from our hometown, and when I answered the call, I did not even recognize his voice; he literally had to introduce himself to me via telephone. I no longer had any interest in him; all of my heartfelt feelings for him were truly dead. God had healed my heart completely from this very devastating experience of a "First Love."

I did not understand this saying back then, but I understand it now: "Be Careful with Your Heart." In other words, "Guard Your Heart." God is really the only one you should truly give your heart to; He is the only one you should give your spirit, mind, and body to. There are some good men out there in the world, and man can have good intentions, but he can also fail you, though maybe not on purpose. Man will at times fail you, but God will never fail you. Trust God, not man. I can truly say that I never felt hatred towards my ex-boyfriend. I felt deeply hurt by him so much so that my heart literally ached. I felt deeply abandoned by him, deeply betrayed by him and I put up a wall in my heart because of him. He had been first in my life.

As a Christian, I had to forgive him for hurting me and love him as God says we must love all people with God's *agape,* which is unconditional love. People, Places, and Things can never be your "First Love," and God must be your "First Love." God is a jealous God and will never tolerate being less than first in your life. God requires our devotion to Him and all others are secondary.

Many years later, while reading the book *Jesus as Counselor* by author Robert C. Leslie, I learned that physicians have discovered that guilt, like anxiety, may serve to inhibit or even paralyze the functions of the body or mind. I also learned that within many of us, emotional feelings create physical conditions that negatively affect our mind and the health of our body. So, I encourage you to ask yourself: do you really have a physical problem, or is it psychosomatic? Do you have emotions such as hurt, anger, or unforgiveness that you consistently carry in your heart toward another person? I wondered if such things could cause otherwise random swellings in the body, as I had suffered from, but at the time when I was suffering from the, I was not even aware of the fact that those emotions were the root of my physical condition of swelling/hives, especially when the seventeen doctors could not medically determine the cause. My grandmother touched on the subject, but of course I ignored her words of wisdom because I felt that I was too strong-willed of a person to allow the situation affect me to that degree.

In chapter five of Robert C. Leslie's book, this chapter titled "Resolving Value Conflicts," I am reminded of the case where a young woman became gradually paralyzed following an accident, even though she had gotten two successful surgical procedures that had given her full use of her legs. But filled with hateful feelings toward her parents, and feeling very guilty because of that hate, she was literally paralyzed by her emotions. When the minister first saw her, she did not believe that God would ever forgive her because of her breaking of the commandment to "honor" her parents. When the minister, in the process of counseling, helped her to accept the forgiveness of God, and eventually to become more accepting and forgiving of her parents' failings, the paralysis eventually disappeared completely.

I now understand that God healed me when I let go emotionally of the situation within my heart. Even though I never felt anger or hate toward my ex-boyfriend, it was still imperative for me to let him go and forgive him of the emotional hurt, disappointment, depression, and feelings of abandonment that I was feeling because of the situation that he created in my life.

I have also learned that Jesus is always walking with us. There were many times when I felt like he was carrying me within his bosom as though I was a six-month-old baby during those times of disappointment, doubt, disillusionment, defeat, discouragement, despondency, depression, and despair, or all the sad D's of life.

Remember, <u>S</u>weet, <u>I</u>nnocent, and <u>N</u>aïve - <u>*SIN*</u> can come in many forms in your life. I pray that you will learn from some of the personal experiences that I have shared with you and avoid <u>*SIN*</u>. Remember, no matter how large or small, sin is still sin. We will never be perfect until Jesus returns, but we can always strive for perfection or maturity, not on our own, but with the help of Jesus Christ, Son of the Living God.

SWEET INNOCENT NAIVE

Scriptures and Spiritual Journal

What To Do When Trouble Hits Your Life
King James Version
Public Domain

(Nahum 1:7 KJV)
The Lord {is} good, a strong hold in the day of trouble; and he knoweth them that trust in him.

(2 Corinthians 4:8-9 KJV)
(8) {We are} troubled on every side, yet not distressed; {we are} perplexed, but not in despair; Persecuted, but not forsaken; cast down, but not destroyed;

(Psalm 138:7 KJV)
Though I walk in the midst of trouble, thou wilt revive me: thou shalt stretch forth thine hand against the wrath of mine enemies, and thy right hand shall save me.

(John 14:1 KJV)
Let not your heart be troubled: ye believe in God, believe also in me.

(Isaiah 43:2 KJV)
When thou passest through the waters, I {will be} with thee; and through the rivers, they shall not overflow thee: when thou walkest through the fire, thou shalt not be burned; neither shall the flame kindle upon thee.

(Romans 8:28 KJV)
And we know that all things work together for good to them that love God, to them who are the called according to {his} purpose.

(Psalm 31:7 KJV)
I will be glad and rejoice in thy mercy: for thou hast considered my trouble; thou hast known my soul in adversities;

(Psalms 121:1-2 KJV)
I Will lift up mine eyes unto the hills, from whence cometh my help. My help {cometh} from the Lord, which made heaven and earth.

(Hebrews 4:15-16 KJV)
For we have not an high priest which cannot be touched with the feeling of our infirmities; but was in all points tempted like as {we are, yet} without sin. Let us therefore come boldly unto the throne of grace that we may obtain mercy, and find grace to help in time of need.

(1 Peter 5:7 KJV)
Casting all your care upon him; for he careth for you.
(Matthew 6:34 KJV)
Take therefore no thought for the morrow: for the morrow shall take thought for the things of it- self. Sufficient unto the day {is} the evil thereof.

(2 Corinthians 1:3-4 KJV)
Blessed {be} God, even the Father of our Lord Jesus Christ, the Father of mercies, and the God of all comfort;(KJV) Who comforteth us in all our tribulation, that we may be able to comfort them which are in any trouble, by the comfort wherewith we ourselves are comforted of God.

(Philippians 4:6-7 KJV)
Be careful for nothing; but in every thing by prayer and supplication with thanksgiving let your requests be made known unto God. And the peace of God, which passeth all understanding, shall keep your hearts and minds through Christ Jesus.

(Isaiah 51:11 KJV)
Therefore the redeemed of the Lord shall return, and come with singing unto Zion; and everlasting joy {shall be} upon their head: they shall obtain glad- ness and joy; {and} sorrow and mourning shall flee away.

Rhema words I personally received from the Lord Spiritual Journal

August 5, 2013 (10:25 a.m.)

Learn to enjoy the present moment in life; allowing your thoughts to run too far ahead in time causes stress in your body, which then causes sickness in your body. Stress is another Trick of Satan to destroy your spirit, mind, and body. Stay in peace by enjoying the moments in life that people take for granted. Take the time to enjoy my creations, take the time to smell my fragrance. Slow down, stop being always in a hurry, you will miss what I am saying and what I am doing. Enjoy life, don't just endure life.

Staying in peace keeps your body healthy, internally and externally. The most beautiful sound is peace and quietness. Learn to tune out the sounds of the world and enter My world of peace and quietness. In the court of the Holy of Holies, that's where you will find Me. Not in the noises of the world.

August 6, 2013 (11:58 a.m.)

Be still and relax. Do not internalize the problems of others. Keep it external so that their problems do not penetrate your spirit. Shake it off and get back into a peaceful mode.

Transferring of spirits is real. This is why you must

be careful of the people you are around. You take on the spirit of others if you do not know how to guard your spirit.

August 7, 2013 (9:20 a.m.)

Remember to always search the scripture for the word on the subject when you have a need or want. Pray My words, believe My word, and you will therefore receive what you prayed for because it is in My word.

My word will never return void. The angels will be busy accomplishing it because My word is true, so it must come forth. The only way My word ceases and the angels stop is that you stop believing and do something out of My will. If you do, quickly repent and what you have prayed for will come forth. It will come from the spirit realm to the natural realm. You shall have what is in My word. Faint not; keep believing until it is manifested. If you feel yourself wavering, say "I still believe no matter what it looks like or feel like, I believe." This is the secret to having what you want or need.

Allow no person, place, or thing persuade you differently than what you believe. That's why you cannot always say what's in your heart of hearts of what you want or need and that you are believing for it, because Satan is always, always listening, and he is always, always plotting to stop the word that you are believing. He will use people, places, and things to stop the Word you are believing.

Rejoice in your heart until the manifestation has

arrived. Remember, Satan will tell you that it will not happen. You tell him that it is written and quote the word back to him and he will flee.

Remember, My Word will create My Will. In order for that to happen, your will must be My Will and nothing can stop it.

August 8, 2013 (10:47 a.m.)

See My creations. I control the ocean, the birds, the mountains, the hills. See the beauty of My creations, that man cannot control. The fish move at My command, the waters move at my command.

I control the clouds and the direction in which they flow; whether they be white or dark, I control. See My touch in all My creations. See the sun, the moon; I determine which will rise. I am that I am, Man has no control.

My creations are submissive to me. Man has a choice to be submissive or not. Those that are submissive are blessed; those that are not, are cursed.

Like the eagle, learn when to soar and when to just be still. My creations represent Me. Everything I have created has a purpose.

My beauty can be enjoyed or despaired, depending on how man use My beauty. The waterfall is beautiful, but only if man use wisdom; My mountains are beautiful, but only if man use them wisely. My oceans are beautiful, but only if man use it wisely; My sun is beautiful, but only if man use it wisely.

Just to watch the beauty of My creations is a heavenly experience until man make the wrong choice and they become a tragedy.

Man can choose Me or Death
Life can be Easy or Hard
My creations are serene. I am that I am, you choose
You choose Day or Night in your life
I am the Day, Satan is the Night

August 9, 2013 (12:05 noon)

Ye are the light of the world. Let your light defeat the darkness of the world by the way you speak, dress, walk, and act. You represent me in this world. I am meek and mild, but I am also bold. Be bold as a lion when you encounter the devil. You cannot be passive. The devil preys on passivity. He's afraid of boldness because he knows he does not have a chance to defeat a bold spirit.

Be kind, but do not be used or taken advantage of. Be discerning of who you can help and of who is trying to manipulate. Manipulation is witchcraft; have no tolerance for it. In the end it will destroy. Do not let the dark put out the light.

This country will come to its knees because of the spirit of manipulation. Many will be lost, but My children will be saved from the disaster that will come. Because I am not first in this country, Satan is their God and the end will mean destruction.

Stay close to the altar, for the destruction will surely come. This country was free when they trusted Me, but when they turned their back on me, they fell into bondage. This country is in a timeline of destruction. Too much acceptance of sin because of money, power and fame. Sin is sin, there is no compromising. There is no fear of Me and no reverence towards Me, and for this purpose, the end will be destruction. When I remove my arms of protection, Satan will have his way. Stay close to the altar.

August 15, 2013 (11:20 a.m.)

Nothing is too good to be true for my children. I am in the blessing business. All my children have to do is ask, believe, and receive; when it is My will, it shall be. All good things are in My will. Do not hesitate to receive what I have already blessed you with. Take it, for it is yours.

Move forward when I say move forward. Blessings come your way daily, and many pass by because you do not always see in the spirit that it is your blessing. Grab ahold of your blessings. Do not allow Satan to stick his ugly head up and steal your blessings. What's yours is yours from Me, but as I did with the Israelites, move when the clouds move, not after they've already moved.

You are in the season of blessings. Grab them, let none of them pass you by. Capture them and hold on to them; do not let them escape or pass you for the next person in line to receive them. This is your season, so seize the moment!

There is a door of opportunity open now! Do not let that door close before you grab your blessings.

August 22, 2013 (9:00 a.m.)

Repenting of sins is the only way to return to Me. When you sin, blessings are put on hold until True Repentance takes place. Let not the sun go down before you repent because you carry the sin to the next in your life. Any amount of time passed without repentance is dangerous for you because it will give Satan the open door to you and destroy you until you return to Me. Quick repentance is necessary, for without it, you give Satan the opportunity to steal, kill, and destroy. His ways towards My people never change. Sin is any person, place, or thing you put before Me. Sin is lust of the eye, lust of the flesh, and the pride of life. I will forgive, but true repentance is required. Remember, I look at the heart and man looks at the outside.

August 27, 2013 (11:50 a.m.)

I am your Strength at all times.

I am your Guide at all times.

I am your Peace at all times.

I am your Joy at all times.

I am your Comforter at all times.

I am that I am, Everything to you and for you. Release Me to be all for you, and I will be in every situation or circumstance in your life.

Keep your inner ears and spiritual eyes open so that you can hear when I speak and see where I should tell you to do.

I will tell you, when, were, why, how, and who. I will direct your path, if you submit all to me. I will not force myself upon you.

Your life will be full of joy, peace, and happiness if you simply give control to Me. I am Everything for you, there is no other.

August 28, 2013 (9:20 a.m.)

Remember, do not take offenses. This is the devil's method of stopping your blessings. Repent quickly and get back in peace. Remember, some people around you are assigned to offend because Satan is their father. They do not understand that they are cursing themselves every time they fulfill their assignment.

Take no thought on what the offender says or does, for they are only cursing and placing themselves closer to the Lake of Fire at the end of their life, and they do not know that. Some know but do not believe their end result, but it will still be the Lake of Fire if they do not repent and give their lives to Me.

Do not respond to them, stay in peace and remember, their end is the Lake of Fire. Their words cannot hurt you, but their words will destroy them.

Remember, offenses stop your blessings and curse the offender.

Pray this prayer: I receive no offenses and I give no offenses. I stay in God's peace.

August 30, 2013 (11:10 a.m.)

Sing a new song unto Me, for it makes Me smile to see you worshipping Me. It convicts the hearts of sinners, it sets the captives free, it heals the broken hearted, it encourages the discouraged. It changes the atmosphere from dark to light, from sorrow to happiness, from defeated to victory. Sing, I say, a new song unto Me.

Those that are lost, will be won; those that are despised, will be embraced. Those that are lonely, will be comforted; those that are sad, will be joyful.

Sing a new song unto Me.

To the readers of this book, may you be blessed, healed, delivered, and set free in the name of the Lord Jesus Christ.

SWEET INNOCENT NAIVE

www.ingramcontent.com/pod-product-compliance
Lightning Source LLC
Chambersburg PA
CBHW071449080526
44587CB00014B/2051